Praise for *Change Yo*

"*Change Your Life with Positive Psychology* is smart, punchy and refreshing. I love all the brilliant insights, exercises and quotes. Pick up this book and enjoy it as you would a cold drink on a hot summer day."

Dr. Ilona Boniwell, founder, European Network for Positive Psychology

"We all want to become the 'best of ourselves' and Charlotte's passionate and inspiring introduction to Positive Psychology is a great place to start. After reading this book you will have the keys to a flourishing, happy life."

Nina Grunfeld, founder, Life Clubs

"This book is more than an introduction to the main ideas within positive psychology; it is a wonderful resource if you are looking to live a happier and more fulfilled life. Clear, succinct and readable, it encourages you to make small adjustments to your life that can really make a difference."

Dr. Anthony Seldon, author, historian and Head of Wellington College

change your life with positive psychology

Charlotte Style

PEARSON

Harlow, England • London • New York • Boston • San Francisco • Toronto • Sydney • Auckland • Singapore • Hong Kong
Tokyo • Seoul • Taipei • New Delhi • Cape Town • São Paulo • Mexico City • Madrid • Amsterdam • Munich • Paris • Milan

PEARSON EDUCATION LIMITED
Edinburgh Gate
Harlow CM20 2JE
United Kingdom
Tel: +44 (0)1279 623623
Web: www.pearson.com/uk

First published in Great Britain as *Brilliant Positive Psychology* in 2011 (print and
electronic)
Rejacketed edition published 2015 (print and electronic)

© Pearson Education Limited 2011, 2015

Pearson Education is not responsible for the content of third-party internet sites.

ISBN: 978-1-292-08335-3 (print)
        978-1-292-08436-7 (PDF)
        978-1-292-08434-3 (eText)
        978-1-292-08435-0 (ePub)

British Library Cataloguing-in-Publication Data
A catalogue record for the print edition is available from the British Library

Library of Congress Cataloging-in-Publication Data
A catalog record for the print edition is available from the Library of Congress

10 9 8 7 6 5 4
18

Series cover design by David Carroll & Co

Print edition typeset in 10/14pt Plantin MT Pro by 71
Printed in Great Britain by Ashford Colour Press Ltd.

NOTE THAT ANY PAGE CROSS REFERENCES REFER TO THE PRINT
EDITION

Contents

Acknowledgements

I would like to thank my husband Charles and daughters Amanda, Annabel and Elizabeth who have given me brilliant support, encouragement and love while I wrote this book. I would also like to thank my wonderful family and friends who are always there and have inspired me to live better. This book is an acknowledgement of all the people I have met along the way who live authentic, full and generous lives.

Publisher's acknowledgements

We are grateful to the following for permission to reproduce copyright material:

Figures

Figure 1.4 from Pursuing Happiness: The Architecture of Sustainable Change, *Review of General Psychology*, Vol 9 (2), p. 116 (Lyubomirsky, S., Sheldon, K.M. and Schkade, D. 2005), APA, adapted with permission; Figure 2.1 (left) adapted from A theory of human motivation, *Psychological Review*, Vol 50 (4), pp. 370–96 (Maslow, A. 1943), APA, adapted with permission; Figure 2.1 (right) adapted from Happiness is Everything, or Is It? Explorations on the meaning of psychological well-being, *Journal of Personality and Social Psychology*, Vol 57 (6), p. 1072 (Ryff, C.D. 1989), APA, adapted with permission.

In some instances we have been unable to trace the owners of copyright material, and we would appreciate any information that would enable us to do so.

CHAPTER 1

What is brilliant about positive psychology

There is not anything in this world, perhaps, that is more talked of, and less understood, than the business of a happy life.

Seneca, 3 BC–AD 62

Positive psychology tells us what works. It is the study of all aspects of living, thinking and behaviour that affect our well-being. Centred on scientific research, positive psychology provides us with evidence of the qualities and skills that significantly contribute to a fulfilling, healthy and flourishing life. It is not just about 'being more positive' but more about becoming the best of ourselves. It is helping us understand and learn how we can experience all areas of our lives better.

The most interesting and relevant research findings wake us up to the power of feeling good, being grateful, thinking positively, acting generously, choosing wisely and being sociable.

Positive psychology is looking much more closely at the many components that contribute to, and go beyond, what is understood as 'self-realisation' and living to your full potential. Positive psychologists speak about a flourishing life.

Positive psychology can tell you:

- What you need in order to feel really motivated
- Why being optimistic is more than just looking on the bright side
- What keeps you living longer and healthier
- The importance and quality of your relationships
- Why you like variety and challenges
- Why you should appreciate what you have
- The importance of accepting yourself

- That having meaning and purpose in your life matters
- Why knowing and using your strengths are important to your happiness
- How life can be as fulfilling as it should be.

Research has shown that becoming richer doesn't make us happier. As long as people are able to pay their bills, their satisfaction with life and happiness does not increase significantly; in fact, over a certain amount of income the level of happiness actually decreases.[1]

However, being grateful for what you have and even giving money away do make you happier![2]

 **example**

Recent research showed that when people were given money, those who were instructed to give it away were happier as a result than those who were free to spend it as they liked.[3]

Background and history

The science of psychology, although originally the investigation of the human mind, has over time applied its knowledge more to naming and fixing what is considered broken or abnormal. 'Positive' psychology is psychology turning back to its roots in looking at the working flourishing mind.

Examining, thinking about and prescribing how to live happily are not new, nor is it new to psychology. Much of the work of humanistic psychology has drawn upon, most notably, the work of Gordon Allport, Abraham Maslow and Carl Rogers. The recent popularity of cognitive behavioural therapy (CBT) and over the past 25 years the growth of life coaching and neurolinguistic programming (NLP) have seen some of the most practical applications of some areas of interest to positive psychologists. Many of the interventions that are integral to all good coaching and self-development practices, such as gratitude, reframing, visualisation, setting meaningful and achievable value-based goals, being attentive, changing mindsets and using strengths, are rooted in psychological and philosophical knowledge.

Positive psychology as a separate and new idea has a purpose. It is bringing together the work of sociologists, anthropologists, clinical psychologists, geneticists, biologists, humanistic psychologists, philosophers and common sense. For the first time there is a united scientific focus examining all that causes us to thrive and flourish, both individually and culturally.

The shelves of bookshops groan with books claiming to improve our lives. Much of what is out there may be backed up by sales but not by serious research. Positive psychology is building a body of evidence that is validating practices and behaviours that really do improve your life. Under this new concept, all areas of research into human flourishing have become united for the first time.

Interestingly, the research findings are beginning to show that many of the range of strategies healthy people use to further their own development are in contrast to many of the mainstream approaches employed among mental health professionals.[4] What works for people when they are mentally unwell, the major focus of psychology in recent years, are not the same strategies used by ordinary and extraordinary individuals dealing with all the good and bad that life has to offer. The strategies and beliefs used by healthy people are much more similar to the key principles and practices advocated by positive psychology.[5]

Legislators, educators, health workers, the business community, the public sector and individuals are utilising the work of positive psychology. There is no area of life that cannot take something from knowing more about what supports human flourishing.

How positive psychology as an idea came to be

'Positive psychology' was born on a beach in New Mexico. It was here that there was a chance encounter between Dr Martin Seligman and Mihaly Csikszentmihalyi, after Seligman responded to hearing someone (who turned out to be Mihaly) in difficulty in the sea and rescued him. After this strange meeting the two men discovered that they were working in the same direction: both were interested in furthering knowledge and reclaiming psychology's interest in the common ingredients of a healthy flourishing life. Csikszentmihalyi was working with the concept of being in 'flow' and Seligman was using his research into learned helplessness to understand better those people who had the capacity to resist and overcome adversity. Positive psychology as a new discipline was born, and the work of psychologists in the following areas, among many others, has become the foundation of this new psychological focus.

The key concepts in positive psychology are:

Optimism

Strengths-based psychology

Flow

Subjective well-being

Psychological well-being

Happiness

Choice

Gratitude

Time perspective

Positive emotions

Emotional intelligence

Goal achievement

Self-acceptance and self-worth

Hope

Resilience

Meaningfulness

Purpose

Wisdom

Spiritual practices.

Change Your Life with Positive Psychology will take you through all of these key concepts, and more, in a way that is accessible and practical to your life. Before we start looking at them, it's important to address what we mean by well-being, how we can quantify it, consider briefly what the research says, and look at a key facet of positive psychology: choice.

The terms of happiness and well being

General well-being is much more than happiness, although, people often use it to refer to happiness. Happiness, well-being and being 'satisfied with life' become intertwined as the best ways to describe a 'functioning' life. 'Subjective' well-being is the best term used to refer to both the cognitive and emotional qualities of 'happiness' and well-being forms the basis of how positive emotion can be measured.

How to measure happiness and well-being

Positive psychology measures everything that affects our quality of life, health and longevity. From having a sense of humour to how good we are at solving problems and recovering from adversity; in fact, there are hundreds of measures and there are many ways in which positive psychologists validate and collate research, even using past evidence. All studies and research that are examining and measuring what affects our happiness and well-being are pertinent to the subject of positive psychology. Positive psychology is the sum of this growing research. At the heart of this research is an analysis of how we choose to act and respond and what traits and factors affect this.

brilliant example

In a study that collated surveys from 45 different countries and over one million people, the positive psychologist Ed Diener took account of all surveys that measured happiness and how satisfied people were with their life and found that the average happiness level on a score from 0 to 10 was 6.75.[6]

The most well-respected and established short measure used to assess subjective well-being is called the Satisfaction with Life Scale (Diener *et al.*, 1985), which consists of five statements (listed below). As you read through them, why not answer them and give a score to each based on the following:

brilliant exercise

Strongly disagree   Strongly agree

1   In most ways my life is close to my ideal
2   The conditions of my life are excellent
3   I am satisfied with my life
4   So far I have got the important things I want in life
5   If I could live my life over, I would change almost nothing

Add the numbers you scored for the five questions to get a total.
See below:

- 31-35 Extremely satisfied
- 26-30 Satisfied
- 21-25 Slightly satisfied
- 20 Neutral
- 15-19 Slightly dissatisfied
- 10-14 Dissatisfied
- 5-9 Extremely dissatisfied

What the research says

Research has found that our genes determine much of our happiness. We are born with a natural capacity for happiness, and some lucky people have more than others. The good news is that we can affect this.[7] This book will tell you what the happiest people are doing and how positive psychology can help you to develop an attitude to living that fosters more opportunities for feeling good and happy.

Happiness is at the heart of well-being because it is such a universal description of feeling good, and experiencing positive emotion is an indication that all is well. It must be remembered, however, that happiness is a by-product; it can elude us if we look too hard for it or if we keep asking ourselves if we are happy. And there are many different ways to be 'happy'.

Nothing is in isolation

There is no one thing that is the key to a flourishing happy life. In fact, research is increasingly showing how integrated everything we do and think is. The only confusion is that because so many things affect our well-being there is always the risk of not trying it all because one thing works.

Almost all happiness and well-being involves connecting our minds, our emotions, our physical bodies *and* our 'souls'. As we enhance well-being in any area of our life we enhance and lighten other aspects of our life.

The interconnectedness of well-being is great because it means that we can each start where it feels good for us. The list below shows some examples of connections and links:

- Exercise affects us physically, mentally and emotionally.
- Feeling good affects how we think as well as our health.
- Emotions facilitate different thinking abilities.
- What we think affects what we feel.
- Learning new things helps us emotionally as well as mentally.
- Those who survived Auschwitz were more likely to be mentally rather than physically strong.
- Spiritual well-being affects us physically.
- The employment of our physical, emotional, mental and spiritual selves to one common purpose expands who we are.

brilliant exercise

Try this. I want you NOT to think about a lemon barley sweet. Don't think about sucking lemon barley for the next two minutes. How is this working?

The mind plays an ironic trick: when we have the thought that we mustn't think about something it sets up a feedback loop that increases, rather than diminishes, in our minds this thing we mustn't think about. Were you able not to think of a lemon barley and did your mouth water, by any chance? When we ruminate on something negative or want to stop doing something that is hard, like overeating or smoking, or even when we just feel miserable and want to stop feeling this way, we can set up such a loop. It is very hard to overcome strong emotion, which can then govern what we think; yet paradoxically what we think may have elicited the strong emotion. Just choosing not to think about the things that make us feel negative may in fact increase these thoughts and feelings, as the above example with the lemon barley sweet shows.

Positive psychology is helping us to understand what we can do to increase positive thinking and feeling, in such a way that it isn't a battle. Fighting and trying to overcome weaknesses and fear, or even imagining that we can never feel negative or angry produces more negativity. Knowing our strengths and using our emotions positively, allows actions and experiences to become easier and happier, both in the short and the long term. We can learn to live more authentically in the whole of our lives, with the 'good' and the 'bad'.

The power of choice

Everything that is the focus and study of positive psychology is relevant to how we live and more importantly informs us how we *choose* to live.

Below are some of the ways you are choosing your experience and well-being; these are some of the factors that govern how and why you make choices, and, in effect, how you choose to think and feel. All these influences are part of your complexity and only you can change or increase what influences your choices.

1 **What you need and value**. You choose what you need. Your basic needs are as individual as you are and what you need are the things that matter most to you, what you value.

2 **As a response**. You choose your response to how others behave and act and to outside circumstances. Someone else's actions affect your choices.

3 **To conform as part of a group.** You choose because it is socially appropriate. You choose to do things you feel you should do because it is considered by others to be the choice you should make. You choose cultural and social norms.

4 **With autonomy.** You choose completely freely and unrestrained. You choose novelty, excitement and uncertainty, for your immediate pleasure.

5 **With your mind**. You choose to do something logically because it makes sense to you.

6 **As a habit.** You choose out of habit. You choose mindlessly, doing what you have always done without thinking about it.

7 **With understanding.** You choose what you understand and is meaningful to you. When you understand *why* you want to do something, you have a reason to choose it.

---

7 ⟩**brilliant** insight

Positive psychology can tell you what the happiest people choose and why.

What are you choosing right now?

Are you awake and open to change?

Are you content and grateful for how much you have or do you want more?

Are you living 'your' life or someone else's and have you chosen this?

Are you choosing to see problems or solutions?

Are you learning from your mistakes or do you feel a failure?

Are you looking forward to the future or does the past hold you in its grip?

Are you choosing safety or adventure?

Are you choosing to be generous with your gifts or do you hold the best of you only for those who deserve it?

Are you choosing to judge yourself and others or are you choosing to see the best in yourself and others?

Let's choose to get going:

- **Chapter 2** will look further at what we mean by happiness and psychological well-being and why the relationship you have with time and choice affects your happiness.

- **Chapter 3** will explore the importance of feeling good, why we should actively seek positive emotion and what the best ways are to start to become happier in a way that lasts and is more fulfilling. It will also help you to find and experience more pleasure in the moment.

- **Chapter 4** will introduce you to your strengths and how you can motivate yourself better and set goals that you really care about.

- **Chapter 5** will explore emotional intelligence and get you thinking about emotions and how you relate to others emotionally.

- **Chapter 6** shares what positive psychology is discovering about being resilient. It takes you through how you think, what you can do to change your thinking, and how optimism and other strategies can help you cope better with both the small and the big things.

- **Chapter** 7 reveals why people who have direction and purpose are much more fulfilled and how to find more meaning and purpose in your own life.

- **Chapter 8** touches on the common attributes of the wise. It will also look at why religious and spiritual people are among the happiest of us and what spiritual practices you can try that will really make you happier.

- **Chapter 9** gets you thinking about being physically well. A healthy mind needs a healthy body.

- **Chapter 10** shares the best positive psychology research in the workplace.

CHAPTER 2

Happiness and psychological well-being

If only we'd stop trying to be happy, we could have a pretty good time.

Edith Wharton, 1862–1937

This chapter will introduce you to what really makes you happy and how a deeper sense of happiness and well-being comes from much more than momentary pleasure. It will look at some of the foundations of your well-being and show that your happiness and ability to flourish depend on six basic psychological needs. It will also look at the effect that your relationship with time has on your happiness and well-being, and why too much choice doesn't make you happier but choosing to be happy might.

Being happy, feeling good, are more than just momentary joy. What makes us 'happy' and what we mean by the term is as individual as we are. Happiness is a by-product of things we do and experience and when we are happy we are more effective both in our own lives and in what we contribute to others. It matters to be happy. It is therefore important that we understand it better.

 **insight**

Knowing what really makes you happy will make you happier than trying to maximise your experience of happiness, which can make you unhappy.[8]

Many people think that the following things are what will make them happy:

- More money
- A nicer house
- Losing weight
- A new car
- New job
- New boyfriend/girlfriend.

Although these things may make a difference to how happy you are, their impact is often short lived. The true sources of happiness and well-being are more subtle and come from both what you *do* and how you *think*.

Two ways to be happy

There are two main distinctions to being happy:

1 **Being happy in the moment,** feeling good, experiencing pleasure and having joy in whatever activity we are presently engaged in.

2 **Feeing 'gratified' and fulfilled,** which is a longer-lasting and more satisfying sense of well-being.

1 Hedonic happiness

The former, 'being happy in the moment', was, in ancient Greece, called hedonic happiness. People who *only* seek happiness this way we speak of as pleasure seekers or hedonists. Being happy and finding pleasure in the moment are wonderful. In fact, all physical pleasure can only really be experienced in the moment. Hedonic happiness is great and is the immediate experience of positive emotions such as joy, pleasure and excitement.

However, the problem with many things that give us immediate pleasure is that they become things we desire for a pleasure that doesn't last. We quickly adapt to having the thing we desired and it no longer gives us the pleasure it did initially. Even winning the lottery boosts happiness for only a short time.[9] We live in a world that exploits this need for immediate gratification and pleasure. This effect is called the ***hedonic treadmill***, forever needing more to feed our voracious happiness habit. Building opportunities for more happiness and positive emotions that **avoids** the hedonic treadmill is the subject of both this and the next chapter.

2 Eudemonic happiness

The second is eudemonic happiness. This is a much more mean-ingful term and contains more lasting and long-term happiness. It implies fulfilment and contentment in relation to well-being. The word eudaimonia refers to the Greek idea of the Daimon, the potential and fulfilment of the true self. Positive psychology has come to the same conclusion as Greek philosophers: that to be **all** that one can be, to fulfil one's potential, leads to fulfilment and happiness.

Many people have argued that the latter kind of happiness is the most rewarding. However, to compare and judge one against the other is to miss the point; we need both immediate and long-term happiness in our lives. Often what gives us pleasure in what we are doing becomes the key that unlocks our ability to seek and achieve better goals and begin to fulfil our potential. When the pleasure in the moment engages us, and when what we enjoy has the capacity to grow and develop in some way, immediate positive emotions become more than a fleeting feeling that fades and dies but can become a resource from which we build and grow. The following chapter will make this clearer.

Unhappiness is caused by desiring what we don't have.

Religion, in particular eastern religions such as Buddhism seek to relieve this by teaching how not to desire.

Western culture seeks to relieve this by trying to satisfy this desire.

The happiness formula

Positive psychologists Sheldon, Lyubomirsky and Schotti have created a happiness formula that breaks down the research into three categories that make up our general happiness (Figure 2.1):[10]

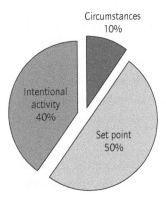

- Your genetic **set point**, S = 50 per cent. This is the capacity for happiness that you are born with.

- The **conditions** of your life, C = 10 per cent. These are both things you can change and things you can't, including your environment, where you live and work, your marriage status, your job, whether you commute or not, and your health and wealth.

- All **voluntary** activities, V = 40 per cent. This includes everything you choose to do for pleasure, both immediate and long term.

Notice that your life conditions hold the least amount of effect on your happiness. Having money or not, good health or not, have far less effect on how happy you are than those things you can choose voluntarily. Sonja Lyubomirsky lists the following things that she and other positive psychologists have found are the most common traits of their **happiest research participants**:

- They have a full and active social life and spend time and effort with their friends and family.
- They are grateful for what they have in life and say so.
- They are generous with their help to others.
- They have a positive outlook.
- They enjoy the present moment and savour life's pleasures.
- They exercise at the least weekly and often daily.
- They hold to their goals and ambitions.
- They have strength and coping skills when they face difficulties, tragedies and adversity.[11]

We will look much more closely at all these traits and practices in the following chapters. Take a moment to see how many of them apply to you.

Happiness and sorrow

We all know people who, no matter what happens to them, find a reason to moan and complain and wish things were otherwise. Equally, we also know people who are always smiling and cheerful. This does not mean we can't be sad. Someone stopped a Buddhist monk who was crying, puzzled at the sight because he believed that practising Buddhism means that you are always happy. The monk replied, 'I am crying because my friend has died.' Sad things make us sad. The chapter on Joy and Sorrow in *The Prophet* by Kahlil Gibran[12] is to me the most profound account of this. Happiness and sorrow come in the same package; what gives us joy also has the capacity to give us pain. Choosing to accept that sorrow and sadness are as much a part of life as happiness and joy is part of well-being. Happy people are able to accept sadness rather than fight against it or deny it. Happy people feel negative emotions too.

Positive psychology is often accused of promoting only the positive and at a glance that may appear to be so, but we will see that there is much more to this 'happiness' business than a simple good and bad approach.

 If you want to understand the meaning of happiness you must see it as a reward and not as a goal.

Antoine de Saint-Exupéry 1900–1944

Happiness as a measure of psychological well-being

Psychological well-being is not happiness, but happiness *is* at the heart of it. Happiness, joy, contentment, fulfilment and excitement are some of the many ways in which we describe feeling good, which is an indicator that all is well, whereas sadness, misery, anger and fear are negative emotions that indicate the opposite.

The confusion comes when we mix up feeling normal negative emotions with negative emotions that indicate we are not flourishing as well as we could be. Psychological well-being is a modern way of describing the Greek idea of eudaimonia, and positive emotions are the by-product of a fulfilled life. Happiness is an important ingredient of a flourishing life but is by no means its definition. Happiness, fulfilment and satisfaction with one's life are a 'measure' of self-realisation and general well-being.

However, we can only really thrive when we are able to fulfil all our basic psychological needs.

The psychologist most well known for listing these needs is Abraham Maslow. Maslow's hierarchy of needs (see below) is still a relevant model, but the model can be extended and reformed; there is more to life than just fullfiling our own needs. People who are really happy are very busy giving back. Actually, there is evidence that Maslow added a sixth need, that of self-transcendence, which includes this requirement for human flourishing, the need to be altruistic, philanthropic and act on empathetic feelings – the need in people to look outside and beyond themselves.[13]

Psychological well-being

Psychological well-being means to be mentally fit and well, as opposed to unwell, and is one of the main assessment measures within positive psychology. According to positive psychologist Carol Ryff, to really thrive and flourish we need to be able to function well in six key ways that, together, constitute and contribute to optimal mental health and living a eudemonic experience of well-being.

Essential components to psychological well-being:

1   Environmental mastery

2   Autonomy

3   A sense of purpose

4   Personal growth

5   Self-acceptance

6   Positive relations with others[14]

There is no hierarchy to them, although they sit well beside Maslow's needs (Figure 2.2). These categories all fall within a very traditional psychological focus on emotional and mental functioning, but they are a good place to start as a checklist that you can tick off and can notice if there are areas of your psychological well-being that might need more attention than others.

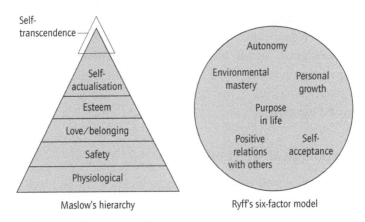

Maslow's hierarchy   Ryff's six-factor model

How strong are the foundations of your psychological well-being?

Happiness and control over your environment

Life is full of challenges, from the everyday skills you require to function and meet your most basic needs to feeling competent in what you do.

A newborn baby is a source of both joy and challenge, but the joy increases as your confidence in your caring skills increases. Similarly, a demanding job becomes more fulfilling when you know you have the skills required to do it. Being a master of your environment requires an ability to handle and organise many activities and make use of opportunities.

Remember the happiness formula: 10 per cent of our happiness is determined by our life conditions. You can't always be a complete master of your circumstances but recognising what you can and can't change is important if you wish to feel more in control of your life circumstances. Do you feel you have control in your life (perhaps you have more control than you think you do), or do you feel you are at the mercy of your circumstances?

brilliant exercise

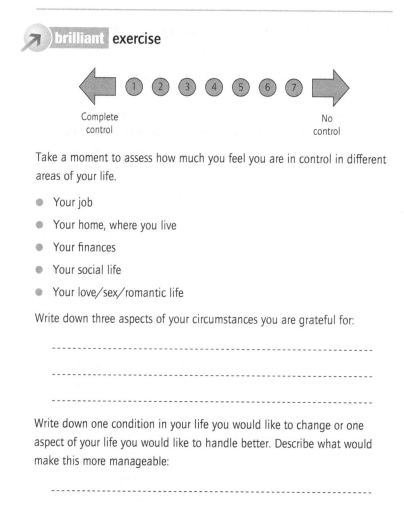

Take a moment to assess how much you feel you are in control in different areas of your life.

- Your job
- Your home, where you live
- Your finances
- Your social life
- Your love/sex/romantic life

Write down three aspects of your circumstances you are grateful for:

Write down one condition in your life you would like to change or one aspect of your life you would like to handle better. Describe what would make this more manageable:

▶ What opportunities do you have right now that can help you manage your circumstances better?

The above questions may help you to focus on how much control you have over your environment.

Remember that you cannot do very much about all the conditions of your life but you can control quite a bit and manage the important circumstances. Control, or at least a sense of control, comes from our technical and cognitive abilities, knowing and accepting those things we can't change and managing and changing what we can.

Having some control and the ability to operate effectively with the conditions in our lives is one way we can affect how happy we are. Our environment is always changing and there are some situations and conditions we can't change, but our view of them can; being able to change your view and perspective is one of the most powerful ways in which you can master your situation.

Do you commute to work? Research has shown that travelling long distances to work affects our happiness and quality of life significantly. Commuting is a known cause of unhappiness; it is a condition that people feel helpless to change. Having no control contributes to unhappiness; traffic jams or late and crowded trains contribute to a sense of helplessness. The effect is so great that people who have received a pay rise and moved away from cramped city living to a nicer house in the suburbs have become unhappier despite better prospects.[15] However, those who see the commuting time as a positive resource, time to make the transition between home and work, time to listen to music or read, are happier.

Happiness and autonomy

Having autonomy means that you are free to choose and able to think independently, whatever the situation. It is important to think for yourself and to be accountable for, and responsible for, the effects of your own actions.

Research demonstrates the effect of having just some control and responsibility. People in a nursing home were given active control over what films they watched, visiting hours, the arrangement of their furniture and a plant to care for, while others had all these things chosen for them and cared for by others. Those who had control were not only happier, and more active and alert, but after two years were also twice as likely to be alive![16]

Autonomy is a major component in being motivated. Having autonomy is thinking for yourself!

Having no autonomy means:

- Relying on the opinions and judgement of others before deciding what to do
- Conforming to social pressures
- Giving up on goals.

Having autonomy means:

- Knowing what you like doing
- Being responsible for your own thoughts and actions
- Being able to think and act independently.

How to build autonomy:

- Set yourself achievable challenges and find someone to support you.
- Don't ruminate and over-think.
- Notice negative thinking about yourself; learn to say 'I can' (see Chapter 6).

● Do more of what you love (see Chapter 4).

● Take responsibility (see Chapter 8).

When you choose to do something for its own sake, for pure enjoyment, you are motivated from within – you are motivated intrinsically. This is a much more motivating force than when you are motivated by an incentive or reward.

Paid incentives increase our motivation to do tasks that don't require us to think; but as soon as the task involves problem solving, paid incentives actually reduce not only our internal motivation but also how well we perform.[17]

---

brilliant example

Children completing jigsaw puzzles saw their motivation reduce when a reward for completing the puzzle was introduced.[18]

This research and many other examples are a demonstration of what is called 'the over-justification effect', when intrinsic, autonomous motivation is undermined by extrinsic reward. Too much reward and too many target-driven incentives can demotivate. (This effect applies only to tasks and activities that involve problem solving and thinking strategies.)

Control is an underlying need! Both autonomy and environmental mastery give us control:

● Autonomy gives us motivation and builds self-reliance.

● Skill and mastery give us active and mental control.

---

brilliant exercise

Being free to think and act of our own volition is a motivating energy that makes us feel good. Answering the questions below will give you some idea of where you feel most autonomy and freedom. All the answers to questions throughout this book are for your interest and as you work through the book you will develop more idea of where your strengths and weaknesses are.

When have you felt most able to be yourself?

When do you feel real freedom of action?

When do you take responsibility?

Have you ever noticed the respect you command when you speak with your own voice?

What are you doing when you feel you have autonomy; what activities do you enjoy for their own sake?

Happiness and purpose

What does it mean to have a sense of purpose? How much would a sense of purpose guide and affect your choices? Having a sense of purpose gives you a reason to aim for something. It encourages you to move towards more fulfilling goals and in doing so enables you to experience eudaimonic happiness as well as a sense of direction and fulfilment. How do you know what it is that you should be doing if you aren't lucky enough to have been given a natural vocation and direction for your life? Finding what you value and knowing what matters to you are a good place to start setting challenges and goals that mean something to you. Having a sense of purpose means having clear goals that fit into and contribute to your wider life story, so that what you do holds some meaning and direction.

- Do you know what your purpose is at the moment?
- What are you aiming for?
- What holds most meaning for you?

We will address this in much greater detail later in this book (see Chapter 7).

Happiness and personal growth

Knowing what means most to you can be realised through personal growth. Personal growth requires that you are open to change and are able to adapt to and cope with all the good and the bad that life deals you. You feel able to achieve your potential and have a sense of continuing development.

Research is showing that having a growth mindset rather than being fixed in how we see the world is an important distinction between people who thrive and those who don't. **People with a growth mindset never stop learning**. Your ability to adapt and learn is a key component of your happiness and well-being. We all face challenges and change, and having an attitude that embraces personal growth happens when we are willing to learn. Setbacks and failure are opportunities to improve and grow. People with a growth mindset love challenges and new experiences.

In her book, *Mindset: The new psychology of success*, Carol Dweck explains how having an open mind to both our abilities and the world we live in allows us to grow and develop, and that holding fixed ideas reduces and limits not only our potential, but our potential for happiness.[19] She also says that as a culture we don't praise enough the effort and struggle people make, especially the young, when facing and overcoming setbacks.

Anyone who has never made a mistake has never tried anything new.

Albert Einstein, 1879–1955

With a growth mindset you:

- Are open to new ideas
- Are always learning (especially from setbacks)
- Enjoy challenges
- Believe that abilities develop
- Believe that lives, relationships and people develop
- Work at relationships

With a fixed mindset you:

- Believe that ability and intelligence are innate
- Are judgemental
- Limit achievment – challenge and adversity scare you
- Believe that if relationships need work they must be wrong
- Believe that if they have to work at things they must be stupid – it should come naturally[20]

↗ brilliant exercise

How open to change and development are you?

Think of a time or incident that was hard for you.

What did you learn?

How did you change?

What in your life has changed for the better because of this?

What, about the experience, are you grateful for?

Types of personal growth:

● **Intellectual growth**, growing in our knowledge of the world
  and developing our reasoning powers

● **Emotional growth**, able to develop emotionally

● **Experience**, able to use experience for positive growth and
  change

● **Self-knowledge**, always finding more about oneself that moves
  towards greater chances of realising one's potential

Research has shown that people with a growth mindset are more
likely to be realistic about themselves and their abilities than
those with a fixed mindset.[21] Being open to growth, learning and
development does not mean an overinflated idea of one's abilities, but openness to possibilities and potential.

⚡ brilliant exercise

Find your mindset

Read the statements below and mark whether you agree or disagree with them:

1 You are the person you are and you can't really change that, or
2 I believe that everybody can change, every kind of person is able to change.
3 The main part of who you are can't change but you can do things differently, or
4 You can always change basic things about the kind of person you are.

[Questions 1 and 3 are the fixed mindset questions and 2 and 4 are the growth mindset.] [22]

If you are most comfortable with statements 1 and 3, try thinking about what it means to you to believe that people cannot change, and, more importantly, what would change in your life if you chose statements 2 and 4. Then:

Make a quick list of where you have opportunities to learn more.

What do you need to learn that would really improve the quality of your life.

Chapter 6 will help you to examine your mindset in greater depth.

Happiness and self-acceptance

Remember that no one is perfect. If you expect others to be saints, it probably means that you should be one too – how hard is that? When you go out to dinner and the meal is delicious, the house is immaculate, the people and conversation amusing and stimulating, the hostess stunningly beautiful, in fact everything is perfect, how much do you want to ask that person back to your house for dinner? The truth is that we like people as much for their frailties, mistakes and weaknesses as for the good things about them, and we also like people who accept us warts and all. Are you seeking to be the perfect hostess in order to like yourself, or do you like yourself warts and all? Self-acceptance is not self-esteem; self-esteem is how you feel, self-acceptance is knowing who you are, valuing all that you are, acknowledging and loving your unique gifts, quirks and failures.

Self-acceptance requires a positive attitude towards yourself. People who need validation and acceptance from other people are more likely to misinterpret other people's responses and reactions. The smallest slight or misunderstanding can mean rejection or overreaction. Being able to accept yourself involves understanding who you really are, both good and bad. We will cover this more in Chapters 5, 6, 7 and 8.

Two important ingredients of self-acceptance are:

1   Having a positive view of the past

2   Not needing outside validation to accept ourselves.

> ● *Do you see your past in a negative or a positive way?*
>
> ● *Do you only feel good about yourself when people praise and love you?*

↗ brilliant exercise

Make a list of things you have achieved for every year of your life from the age of ten.

Try to think of at least one challenge you faced and overcame, or something you did that was positive, for each year of your young life. The reason this is important is that we often take our childhood idea of ourselves into adulthood and what we see as weak from a child's perspective can be the very opposite. Try to think of achievements that you may not have recognised at the time as well as listing what you did achieve. Try to find ways in which you were creative as well as able. If you find this difficult, get someone else to help you.

Happiness and positive relations with others

Getting on with other people, communicating and feeling connected and related in some way is one of our most basic needs. Your success or otherwise at relationships is a source of both hedonic and eudaimonic happiness and well-being and is vital to your mental health.

A universal torture or punishment is to isolate people.

↗ brilliant insight

The most common factors among the happiest people are a full and active social life, good friends and a current romantic partner.

The happiest people are sociable people, but it is not clear from research whether people with good relationships are very happy people, or if people who are very happy have good and satisfying relationships.[23] Having close friends, family support and a romantic partner affects not just your mental health but your physical well-being, your general health and your mortality.[24]

The psychologist Michael Argyle lists three sources of satisfaction in all relationships that meet our basic relational needs:

- Instrumental help
- Emotional support
- Companionship.

He also notes that the most important relationships in our life change over time. As children it is with our parents, in adolescence it is friendship followed by romantic and loving partnership, and finally in later life friendships are again most important.[25]

Quality of relationships matters more than quantity
Having close friends you can trust is what will make you happiest. It is better to have fewer good friends than many acquaintances.

Being happily married is a huge factor for happiness, health and well-being, and happier than cohabiting.[26]

Getting on well with other people requires empathy, the ability to trust people, a caring approach to others and emotional intelligence. People who are loving, cooperative and open are more likely to enjoy intimacy and life satisfaction.[27] If you are not able to share and be open about yourself, you will find it harder to enjoy meaningful and intimate relationships.

We trust people who trust us, we care about people who care about us.

Almost all our interactions with others involve some form of reciprocity; we give what we get – both good and bad. The psychologist Jonathan Haidt believes that reciprocity is embedded in us, not just because we like to give what we receive but because we judge each other and keep people socially accountable by our approval or disapproval.

↗ **brilliant** insight

We are so wired to reciprocate that in an experiment psychologist Phil Kunz received 117 Christmas cards from 578 strangers to whom he sent cards with his address on them wishing them a happy Christmas – he even got onto the permanent Christmas list of some.[28]

If this is how we are wired, what is stopping you from being the first to connect? Give what you wish to receive.

- How much do you give of yourself to others?
- Do you have close trusting relationships in your life?

Chapter 5 is all about positive relationships and improving your emotional intelligence and communicating skills. We will cover this subject in full there.

We have examined briefly six key components that are vital to your psychological well-being and potential to flourish. We will now look at two other factors important to your well-being and happiness: time and choice.

Happiness and time

Being *present* in your life is one of the key ways you can enjoy your life more and in the next chapter we will discover this further. However your well-being and happiness are also affected by your relationship to the past, present and future.

Imagine you are a glass of water that also contains sand. Every time the sand in the glass is shaken up it stops you feeling good. What shakes the glass up is moving about. This movement can be forwards, backwards, or sideways. Forward movement represents thinking about the future, which can elicit either apprehension or anticipation. Backward movement of the glass represents thinking about the past, which can be either nostalgic or stressful. Sideways movement represents comparing yourself with other people, to the right positively, being glad that we are better off than 'them', and to the left negatively, wishing to be like 'them'. Every time our thoughts are in any of these places, the glass is dancing about, and the sand is clouding the water. We think and feel better with a

▷

> clear glass. Of course, we move in all these directions but when we are moving in large circles it is harder to be happy.
>
> *How big a dance circle are you engaged in?*

Your well-being is compromised when you are too focused towards only one time perspective. You need to be able to combine your time perspectives to include a healthy relationship to the past and spend time enjoying the present with one eye on the future.

Happiness and hedonism

Being present is very important but you also need to be healthily engaged with the past and the future. If we focused only on pleasure in the moment we would be rampant hedonists, indulging our every whim at the expense of tomorrow. Sitting exams, doing mundane chores or staying in a relationship after the first excitement has worn off would never happen. The hedonist's life is one where there is no purpose, no goal, *other* than seeking pleasure in the present moment, and the idea of working or putting effort into something that will give positive emotion in the future is counter to that goal. Having the ability to delay gratification and pleasure is essential to any normal existence. In fact, the ability to delay gratification is a well-known attribute of 'successful' people.

brilliant insight

Research by psychologist Walter Mischel is a famous example of delayed gratification.

A marshmallow was given to children and then the children were told that if they didn't eat it and waited five minutes they would get two marshmallows. Fifteen years later the children who had shown that they could delay gratification and were able to control their desire were much more successful than those who gave in and ate the marshmallow.[29]

Being able to delay gratification is a good thing, but not at any cost. We can all recognise the flaws in stereotypical hedonistic behaviour. We can visualise people who live indulgently and suffer the consequences. But it can mean that in our efforts to avoid the hedonistic trap, we can become **too** focused on the future, working ourselves into the ground for a future pleasure when we may die before we get to enjoy it. Always saving for a future rainy day at the expense of enjoying the sun today.

In their book, *The Time Paradox*, psychologists Philip Zimbardo and John Boyde tell us that having the right time perspective has an enormous effect on how we feel. Whether we are predominantly past, present or future orientated profoundly affects our happiness and well-being. You can see Philip Zimbardo talking about this at www.tedtalks.com in his short summary or visit his site, www.thetimeparadox.com.

brilliant insight

The time perspective we hold has been linked to many choices and behaviours:

- Who and when we marry
- Health choices
- Sexual behaviour
- How likely we are to drink or take drugs.[30]

Negative or positive time perspectives

Past perspectives

If you have a **positive perspective of the past,** you have happy memories and a positive identity shaped by a healthy and happy childhood and past experiences.

If you have a **negative perspective of the past**, you see the past as full of bad experiences, and unhappy and regretful memories have shaped your identity.

brilliant insight

Philip Zimbardo has found that people who are strongly past positive have much more meaning in their lives than those who have a negative view of the past. A strong past perspective affects well-being more than any other time perspective.

The sand in the glass gets shaken up when we are focused *only* on the past, which allows the past positive person to become nostalgic and the past negative person to be fearful and haunted.

Present perspectives

If you feel good and enjoy what you are doing and you are fully present, if you love the joy of life and are someone who loves living in the moment, finding excitement and pleasure, you are a **present hedonistic person.**

brilliant insight

Having a positive present time perspective is a contributing factor to well-being and satisfaction with life.[31] Being present hedonistic gives you opportunity to experience more positive emotions such as joy and excitement, which we will see in the next chapter is important to your well-being.

If you feel you have no control over your life, if you feel helpless and resigned to the winds of fate blowing you where they will, you are a **present fatalistic person**.

To be focused *only* on the present allows the hedonist to be unrestrained and the fatalist to have no reason to engage with life or choose any autonomous action.

Future perspectives
If you are a **future-orientated person** you have goals and a purpose and direction in your life.

🔁 brilliant insight

Research shows the future-orientated person as being more optimistic and successful.

Someone who is focused *only* on the future is delaying gratification at the expense of relationships, hobbies and even health. To be *too* focused on the future shakes up the glass when you are either fearful or over-anticipatory. In order to have a clear glass that gently sways forwards and backwards without shaking up the sand, we need to have temporal awareness that includes *all* positive time perspectives.

Optimal time profiles
Philip Zimbado believes that there is an optimal profile, which is:

- **Highly past positive** because this gives us roots and identity.
- **Moderately highly future orientated** because this is how we seek challenges and goals.
- **Moderately present hedonistic** because pleasure in what we are doing energises us.

If you would like to test your own time perspective profile, you can do so online with the Zimbardo Time Perspective Inventory.

> *Note* The emphasis on being **past positive** mirrors Ryff's findings on healthy self-acceptance, which is also dependent on a positive attitude to the past.

If you don't have a positive feeling towards the past, it might be for a good reason. For now, just notice that this is what you think and that having this thought may be affecting how you enjoy life in the present. There will be plenty of opportunity in later chapters to find ways to accommodate and find meaning and benefit in all experiences. **For now, don't feel any pressure to do more than just notice.**

- What is your predominant time perspective?
- How might this be affecting your happiness and enjoyment of life?

A flexible and balanced time perspective starts with noticing your relationship to time and how you use it.

Happiness and choice

Our happiness is greatly affected by how much choice we have and the manner in which we choose. This is not the same as the underlying needs and motivations that govern all our actions and behaviours that we touched on in the last chapter; choice in this context is much more about the practical way we choose.

Too much choice is not good for us!

In a series of studies, people who were given the chance to sample jams and chocolate were more likely to buy when they had only six to sample than when they had to choose from 24 or 30.[32]

Changing your mind doesn't make you happy

After being asked to choose only one of two meaningful photographs as a keepsake of their time at university, the group of students who had a minute to choose and were not allowed to change their minds were happier with their choice a year later than those who had been given a three-month delay before making their final choice.[33]

According to the psychologist Barry Schwartz there are two types of choosers: maximisers and satisfiers.[34]

The agony of maximising choice

If you are a maximiser, you will spend hours assessing and comparing all options, trying to find the right choice that maximises all scenarios. If you are choosing shoes, for instance, you will try on every pair of the style you want in your price range before making your purchase on the grounds of value for money, comfort, fashion and utility. You will probably make a very well-informed decision but you are also less likely to be completely satisfied.

What is it like to live as a maximiser with the amount of choice we have around us today? Shoes or a healthy yogurt are simple commodities to choose compared with where you live, what car you drive, what career you choose, what insurance you need, where you want to go on holiday, what school you send your children to or who you spend your life with. Looking at all the options is not only exhausting and time consuming but if, after investing all the time and effort, you make a wrong decision, regret and self-reproach can be a further burden to bear.

The joy of being satisfied

If on the other hand you are a satisfier, choosing is a more functional action, decision making reflects current needs, and options help to meet the minimum requirement. Satisfiers may not make as good decisions as maximisers but they are more content with their choices and happier.

● Are you a maximiser or a satisfier?[35]

Limiting the negative effects of maximising

If you care too much what other people have and are doing, or you are a perfectionist, or you always want to get the best option, you are probably a maximiser and would benefit from the following:

● Try to accept a 'good enough' approach to your life.

● Stop comparing what you have with what other people have.[36]

● Lower your expectations.

● Enjoy what you have.

● Stick to what you have chosen, especially the small things.

● Limit your choices when you can.

Maximising is not all bad; taking time and consideration is sometimes important and there are decisions in our lives that require proper reflection and attention. The important thing to learn – whether you are a maximiser or a satisfier – is when it is beneficial to invest time and trouble in your choices and when it is detrimental. Try the 'So what?' question. Give things a score of 1–10 on a 'So what?' or 'How much does it matter?' scale.

Maximisers are more likely to suffer

● Depression

● Regret

● Lost opportunities.[37]

Having too much choice impedes our happiness and well-being. In his book, *Affluenza*, Oliver James describes the effect that consumerism and choice are having on people as an affliction that causes people to be not only unhappy but ill.

brilliant recap

This chapter has introduced you to some of the important aspects and factors in your happiness and psychological well-being. It has explained that:

● Happiness can be both immediate and lasting.

● There are things that we enjoy as pleasure in the moment but we must beware of desiring things that give us only short-term pleasure.

● To really flourish you need six fundamental abilities as foundations to your well-being and happiness:

  1 Mastery of your environment: means you can affect and control the circumstances of your life.

  2 You are responsible for your thoughts and actions, you can think and act for yourself.

  3 You have purpose and direction in your life.

  4 You have the opportunity and mindset to grow and develop.

  5 You accept and like yourself.

  6 You have positive relationships and social connections.

● Your happiness is affected by your relationship to time.

● Your happiness is affected by too much choice.

CHAPTER 3

How to build positive feelings and become happier

The happiness of life is made up of minute fractions. The soon forgotten charities of a kiss or a smile, a kind look, a heartfelt compliment – countless infinitesimals of pleasure and genial feelings.

Samuel Taylor Coleridge, 1772–1834

This chapter will build on the last by explaining the importance of happiness and positive emotions. It will get you to start thinking about what you enjoy and how you can find more pleasure in the everyday. It will tell you what are the best long-term happiness boosters, introduce you to what it means to be in flow and remind you of the joy of living attentively in the present.

Positive feelings, or positive emotions, are much more than just feeling happy. Positive feelings include: joy, pleasure, excitement, surprise, delight, interest, fun, pride, love, desire, awe, wonder, contentment, enjoyment and, of course, happiness. Feeling positive emotion is vital to our well-being, not just for the good feeling it gives us but also as an agent in our personal growth, development and health.

The things most likely to give us immediate joy and pleasure are:

- Eating
- Social activities
- Sex
- Exercise and sport
- Alcohol and other drugs
- Success and social approval
- Use of skills
- Music and all the arts
- Religion

- Good weather
- A great environment
- Rest and relaxation.[38]

The importance of positive emotions

Positive psychology is showing us just how dynamic the effect of positive emotion is.

Feeling positive emotions literally opens our minds. It makes us more creative and becomes part of an internal feedback loop that creates an upward spiral towards **more** positive emotion. The psychologist Barbara Fredrickson calls the effect of positive emotion on our development and ability 'the broaden-and-build theory'. For Fredrickson, positive emotions are essential elements of optimal functioning and human flourishing; positive emotions broaden the mind, making us better at living.[39] Feeling good has a beneficial effect that builds our intellectual, social, psychological and physical abilities.[40]

The happier we are, the better people we become!

Positive emotions are a powerful resource. They build and support:

- Confidence and self-belief
- Creativity, originality and flexibility
- Physical and mental health
- Intellectual ability
- Intuition and perception
- Optimism
- Perseverance
- Productivity, activity and energy
- Recovery from illness and reduction of pain

- Health and how long we live
- Better relationships and social skills, connection and communication with others
- Better coping with challenges and stress
- Ability to help others
- Ability to overcome negative emotions: when we are happy it is hard to be sad.[41]

Feeling good makes you think better in order to build more good feeling!

Positive emotion as a positive resource

When we feel joy, pleasure or any positive emotion, it is stored in our memory bank. This is a vital resource from which we can draw positive feelings and emotions from the past, to help us in the present. Wanting to repeat the pleasure or emotion helps us to grow and develop by seeking it again, or using it to expand the experience. Happy people are more likely to attempt new activities and goals when feeling good, and they have more skills and resources to draw on from past activity while feeling good.[42] When we are happy we are better able to react and respond to our environment, which in turn builds more resources. This in turn builds more self-belief, ability and further action and positive emotion.

 **insight**

Just as negative emotions have a role in adapting our behaviour and building our survival strategies – 'fight or flight' – so do positive emotions, adapting us to positive development and creative ability.

Positive emotion: an instigator for creativity and development

- **Joy** sparks the urge to play, which encourages social development.

- **Interest** sparks the urge to explore, to learn.

- **Contentment** sparks the urge to savour and integrate.

- **Love** sparks us to want to explore these things within close relationships.[43]

brilliant example

In a study by Fredrickson and Branigan, participants were shown films that induced either positive or negative emotions. Immediately after the film clips, their ability to list things they would like to do at that moment was tested. Those who experienced joy were able to think of twice as many things as those who had experienced anger.[44]

brilliant insight

We need a minimum of three times more positive emotion than negative in order to flourish. The actual magic number is 2.9.[45] Any less than this is not effective. This ratio is like a tipping point. Being a bit more positive than negative has no effect; only over the 2.9 ratio do people flourish. This is not to say that we can or should try to feel good all the time; the three-to-one ratio allows space for negative emotions. Flourishing is also curtailed by too much positivity; scientists have found that flourishing breaks down once the ratio reaches eleven to one.[46]

Real life is a mix of many emotions. The trick is to learn how to boost your ability to feel good at least three times more often than bad, and then get into the habit of doing it.[47]

Building positive feelings: how to increase lasting positive emotion

Feeling good is not forced jollity. It is much more about being totally present to all the good things around us, learning to find more things that make us feel good and becoming more appreciative of those opportunities. We feel best when we are able to be fully ourselves, even in difficult circumstances. Here are five brilliant ways in which you can bring more opportunity for feeling good almost immediately and that will also give you pleasure that lasts.

1 Be open and curious – open your mind

Let go of rigid expectations. We will return to this subject throughout the book because it is so important. Being open to new (and old) experiences and open to continuous learning, having a growth as opposed to a fixed mindset, has a great effect on every aspect of your happiness and well-being.

How can you become more open to your immediate experiences? Your expectations shape your experience and therefore your pleasure. If you expect something to be bad it probably will be, and if you expect something to be great you may experience disappointment when it is not.

How can you become more curious? Curiosity does more than broaden your mind; curiosity is a significant factor in well-being. Research has proved that the more curious we are, the happier we are, both in our pleasure and joy in the moment and in our general well-being.[48] The psychologist Todd Kashdan calls curiosity the 'engine of wellbeing'.[49] Knowing who you are, what you enjoy, how your life can be better, safer, happier or easier is the beginning of making it so. The more curious you are, the bigger your world gets, and your knowledge of yourself, others and the world deepens.

Anxiety can be cured with curiosity. Next time you feel anxious you may notice that it is because there is something you don't know, so:

● Say you don't understand
● Find out what you need to do
● Get curious about why you are anxious.

The more open you are to new ideas and perspectives, the more you will get from the ideas in this book and the more you will be able to affect your happiness and well-being.

↗ **brilliant** impact

Decide today to be open and curious to any and all possibilities and to let go of any attachment to specific outcomes.

---

2 **Be grateful and appreciate what you have** – open your eyes

What are you grateful for? Probably one of the most important ways to increase your day-to-day pleasure and happiness is to appreciate what is good in your life and to appreciate some of the things that you may take for granted.

Appreciating your life will boost your well-being in all areas of your life. Of all the findings in positive psychology, the effect of gratitude is immense, and being grateful will also be a recurring theme throughout this book. Sometimes we just forget to notice all we have.

Being grateful is one of the healthiest positive emotions, and makes you more:

● Alert

● Enthusiastic

● Determined

● Attentive

● Empathic

● Kind

● Happy

● Healthy.

Research by Robert Emmons and Michael McCullough shows that writing on a weekly or daily basis about the things you are grateful for can:

● Make you healthier

● Encourage you to exercise

● Help you towards achieving personal goals

● Make you more optimistic.[50]

brilliant exercise

Why not try keeping a gratitude journal? In their research Emmons and McCullough used the following instruction: 'There are many things in our lives both large and small that we might be grateful about. Think back over the past week and write down up to five things that happened for which you are grateful or thankful.'

▷

▶ This week I'm grateful for: _____

_____

_____

_____

_____

_____

_____[51]

The effects of expressing gratitude regularly:

- You recover from illness better and faster.
- You cope with stress better.
- You are more inclined to be moral.
- Your relationships get better.
- You want and desire less, and are happier for longer with what you have.
- You feel greater self-worth and higher self-esteem.
- You experience fewer feelings of anger, guilt and jealousy.[52]

Knowing what you appreciate and are grateful for will also remind you to say so to other people!

 **impact**

Thank someone personally. One of the most effective positive interventions is to write a letter to someone you wish to thank and to deliver it personally. To get the full benefit, read out loud what you have written to the person to whom it is addressed. This is a hard thing to do and socially unusual, to say the least. However, the effect is a genuine long-lasting 'feel-good factor' for both the recipient and the giver.[53]

3 **Be kind** – open your heart

A while ago someone put an ad in a newspaper inviting people to join a club; it didn't say anything about what the club did, it was purely an invitation to join a club. Amazingly, people applied and the club was born. This response prompted the need for the club's purpose, which became 'doing a random act of kindness on Friday'. We can act this way without joining a club; just put it on your list and see what happens and how this makes you feel. There are many initiatives that promote random acts of kindness.

▶ brilliant example

In a ten-week experiment Sonja Lyubomirsky asked people to practise random acts of kindness. What was interesting about this research was that the effect on happiness depended on the **variety** and not the frequency.[54]

In another study in Japan people were asked to count their kindnesses. The results showed that happy people became more kind and grateful, and all participants became happier.[55]

You can increase your positive emotion and well-being by increasing your kindness. One of the ways you can do this is to practise a loving kindness meditation. In recent research, practising a loving kindness meditation has been shown to improve relationships, health and well-being.[56]

Remember that we are wired to reciprocate, so why not start the pendulum and give someone something you would like to be given to you? Random acts of kindness can be anything: something as simple as thanking someone, or stopping to allow a car to pull out in front of you or letting someone onto a train before you. All random acts of kindness are a real boost to happiness.

The child psychologist Bernard Rimland, director of the Institute for Child Behavior Research, found that 'the happiest people are those who help others'. In his study, people were asked to list ten people they knew and then to mark each according to how happy they thought they were. They were then asked to rate the same people for how selfish they were. Those who were less selfish were also more likely to be the happiest.[57]

Why not try this experiment for yourself? Rimland's criterion for selfish behaviour was 'a stable tendency to devote one's time and resources to one's own interests and welfare - an unwillingness to inconvenience one's self for others'.

🡕 ❨brilliant❩ impact

Get inventive with your kindness. It is very important to remember how much **variety matters**. We love surprise, so keep your kindness fresh.

4 Be with other people

We have already seen that being with other people is one of the greatest sources of happiness and immediate pleasure.

- How much time do you spend with your friends?
- How much time do you spend with your family?

Making time for friends and family involves picking up the phone and getting out the diary, but sometimes it just means saying no to something else. Research will tell you that if you have enough money to pay your bills and you have a choice between making an extra £1,000 over the weekend or spending that time with family or friends, you will be much much happier if you choose friendship.[58]

Making time for old friends is important but getting out and making new friends also matters. As you change and develop in your life, different people share with you your different needs and interests. If your social life is looking a little flat, what can you do about it today?

brilliant insight

Children have so much to teach us about feeling good. We laugh when we are children much more than as adults and children know how to play and be curious. If you have children you have an immediate source of a happiness boost.

5 Be real – open yourself

Allow your true nature to shine! Martin Seligman, the 'father' of positive psychology, talks a lot about being authentic and we will return to this subject in the following chapters, 4, 5 and 7 especially. Being real is knowing who you are at your best and happiest, and living in 'your' skin. You will find yourself being real when you are happy and you are happiest when you are able to be all that you are.

We now have five happiness boosters that will start you spiralling upwards, but what if all you need at the moment is an immediate way to boost your mood and enjoy your life more? If you are not a natural hedonist it is probably time to increase your joy and pleasure in living.

Make a list of all the activities that give you an immediate positive feeling, and then score each activity in two ways: for the amount of pleasure it gives you and how much this activity is currently in your life. Use a scale of 1 to 10 in each case, with 10 being the most and 1 being the least. When you have done this, review your list and think about the differences between each score.

Now think back to past pleasures and make a list of things you used to enjoy.

Why did you love doing this?

And why have you stopped?

What pleasures are you making time for?

What pleasure would you like to make time for?

What are you doing when you lose track of time?

Finding flow

What are you doing when you lose track of time?

Are there activities that cause you to become oblivious to everything else around you?

When are you really engaged and excited such that nothing else matters?

Positive psychologists talk of being 'in flow'. Flow is the experience of being so engaged with what you are doing that you became unaware of everything else – even time. Having flow in your life is a major source of both immediate pleasure and overall well-being. Mihaly Csikszentmihalyi, one of the founders of positive psychology, describes this experience as being in flow because the experience is so effortless.

Csikszentmihalyi says you are 'in flow' when you:

- Are using your key strengths to overcome a challenge
- Have clear goals which are distinctly defined
- Are fully concentrating
- Are focused only on the task at hand and are aware of nothing else
- Have a sense of control
- Lose track of time
- Are doing something for its own sake.[59]

Flow is one of the most pleasurable states we can experience; when we are so lost in what we are doing that we become oblivious to everything else, all our cares and worries fall away, even time.

How to get flow in your life

1 *Develop old and build new skills*

In flow the enjoyment of the activity is closely related to the ability: the more skill and ability, the greater the reward. It is this that pushes people both to do more and to push themselves further. Learning new skills is a great way to increase flow in our lives, and with more flow comes more pleasure, happiness and life satisfaction.

Can you think of a new skill or development of an existing skill which would give you the opportunity to be in flow? If you have experienced being so engaged in what you were doing, what skill were you using?

2 *Aim for excellence*

Getting really good at a skill will give you both the pleasure of the skill and also the pleasure of achievement. Sportsmen and women talk of being in 'the zone', of experiencing 'peak performance'. There is a complexity to anything that requires both a level of skill and the opportunity to become expert. Complexity satisfies and gives the experience perpetual novelty.

3 *Seek challenge*

When do you enjoy being challenged? Where can you increase and develop your skills with more challenges? Flow happens when you are using a skill, which you can improve. You need challenges for your skills to flourish. Any task becomes more enjoyable if you add a challenge. Can you do it better, faster or neater?

Flow is most often experienced during an activity that you have chosen to engage with, such as sport, playing music, being creative and any challenging physical activity. However, it is possible to be in flow in any activity where a skill meets a challenge.

Flow can be so pleasurable that we can often become addicted to an activity that produces it. Many computer games fulfil the criteria for generating flow in this way, but remember that it is healthier in the long term to find flow in worthwhile and meaningful activities.

The importance of skill and challenge

When people are in flow things are almost effortless, there is a sense of being in total control and yet there is an edge to this. The balance between skill and challenge is tenuous. The challenge must be enough for the skill to meet and match it; too much challenge and the experience is out of control. The challenge in the activity must always be pushing at this edge in order that your attention is brought to the task in hand; too little challenge and your mind can wander or become bored.

4 *Do what you love, use your strengths*

Do things you are good at and love. If you have ever experienced flow you were probably using one of your top strengths. We learn about strengths in the next chapter.

5 *Be totally focused*

Writers and artists talk of the 'creative juices flowing' and say that the work is almost creating itself. Being this immersed in something, concentrating at such a level, denies any thought of past or future; when in flow one is totally focused in the present moment to the exclusion of everything. Being so focused on something that involves all your concentration and attention, so that the whole of you is involved and you almost become one with the activity, is to be in flow.

6 *Have a clear goal*

Being focused on a clear intent is also central to being in flow. Know exactly what you are trying to do. Ask yourself what the purpose and point are of what you are achieving.

brilliant insight

Research has shown that flow supports and benefits:

- Creativity
- Peak performance
- Talent development
- Productivity
- Self-esteem
- Stress reduction
- Psychological well-being.[60]

Not to be engaged in what we are doing is to be more than just bored; the opposite of flow is apathy. Work can easily become boring and frustrating for people doing repetitive easy tasks that require little or no skill or concentration. It is only extrinsic motivation such as paid incentives that offers a reward-like goal. It is not hard to see that when people enjoy their work, it is because there is some part of it that stretches the mind or they can improve their skills and abilities.

- Can you think of opportunities to experience flow?
- What on your list are things that involve both skill and challenge?
- How can what you are doing right now be more engaging; can you do it better, faster or neater?
- What aspects of your tasks today can you develop more skill doing?
- Aim for excellence!

Flow experiences are a great way to discover your strengths and skills, and being in flow is also a way to be fully present.

Becoming present

We experience the world through our senses. We see, hear, touch, feel and taste. Our senses are our physical experience of the world; philosophers have argued, and are still doing so, that our minds are only subjects of the senses.

Physical pleasure is felt in the present, and is experienced through the senses: all experiences can be remembered, and certainly can be anticipated. Physical experience can only be 'felt' in the present but is part of an emotional experience when we engage our minds and are fully cognizant.

 **exercise**

Why not bring yourself into your present sensual experience?

- Right now, what good feelings are you experiencing through your senses?
- Are you comfortable?
- What are your surroundings?
- Can you see something that is beautiful?
- What can you hear?

Now remember recent sensual pleasures.

- When did you last eat something delicious?
- How do you feel when you hear your favourite music?
- When did you last dance with abandon?
- What was your last sexual experience like?

Thinking about these questions has hopefully made you think about what you find sensually pleasurable and made you feel more present. All sensory joy is momentary; pleasure and happiness come upon us fleetingly. They ebb and flow but are something we constantly seek and recognise. Practising becoming more present helps you open your **mind** to your senses and your surroundings. Allowing time for sensory pleasure is important to our well-being. Being present to pleasure also allows you the ability both to recollect past pleasures and to anticipate future pleasures. Positive psychology is shedding light on how people who enjoy and take pleasure in life in the present are better able to anticipate the future positively.

How to become more present

One of the best ways to become more present is to savour.

Savouring

The first two things you can do is to **notice** and to be **present**. Start by becoming more engaged and focused on what you are doing, on what is directly in front of you **right now**.

brilliant tip

> To increase your physical experience, take time to pause and connect with what is around you, to notice fully your surroundings, your body, and to look for and see beauty. Savouring is a process, not an outcome; it is something we **do**.

In their book, *Savouring*, psychologists Fred Bryant and Joseph Veroff describe savouring as '*the capacity to attend to, appreciate and enhance positive experiences in one's life*'.[61]

In many religious and spiritual practices, being focused on the task in hand is either prayerful or meditative. For positive psychology the focus on savouring is not dissimilar. Savouring means to be **really** present to what and where you are.

Great ways to savour

- Slow down.
- Share what you enjoy with other people; bring others into your pleasure in the moment.
- Really notice the details. Become fully absorbed in what you are doing so that even things that are familiar become almost new. Try to see something as if for the first time.
- Celebrate the moment, if it is that kind of a moment! Get excited. Laugh, shout, and jump for joy. People at sports events are not just in the excitement of the game; the experience is heightened by the number of people all expressing the

thrills and spills wildly and publicly. Live concerts are also remembered and enjoyed as much for the joy expressed as for the performance.

- Commit things to memory with a photograph, descriptive written account or a memento. This is great way to re-savour past experiences.

- Make it last, draw out the experience, take time over things to relish and enjoy with greater understanding.

- Be grateful for what is around you and who is with you.

- Use your senses! Taste, smell, listen and touch.

- Let food linger in your mouth.

- Open your ears to the background hub of life.

- Bring your attention to listening with a more singular focus.

- Feel your clothes.

- Touch as well as look at a leaf or flower, really feel the textures around you.

- Dance with abandon.

- Taste as if for the first time.

- Look with wonder and curiosity.

brilliant tip

Don't be too deep and heavy; pleasure is most exquisite when it unfolds of its own accord – all you have to do is be awake to it!

There are two aspects to savouring:

1 The *type* of experience – what is felt through either the mind or the senses

2 The *focus* of attention – either an external focus, something around us on which we are presently focused, or an internal focus; the memories we are able to recollect and enjoy internally that originated as an external pleasure.

Both these aspects can be of the mind or the body. Being fully awake to life engages both your body and your mind.[62]

 **insight**

Pleasure and happiness are found when we aren't worrying or analysing whether or not we are happy. The pleasure, the happiness, the enjoyment are simply to be fully engaged in something we love. When we are fully engaged we don't even notice time passing.

Feeling good in and beyond the present moment ... lasting pleasure

We have seen that feeling good is beneficial to us in a number of ways. The pleasure and positive emotion that any activity generates will be longer-lasting when it engages the mind. More gratifying than short-term mindless physical pleasure in the moment are pleasure and happiness that last beyond the moment because they were consciously experienced and enjoyed.

brilliant exercise

Why not keep a diary of activities that change your mood. Think about:

● Where you can put more positive emotion in your day?

● Count your kindnesses.

● Notice what you are grateful for.

● How can you become more open and curious?

- How can you savour your life more?
- Set aside time with friends and family.
- List things that make you feel good.
- Make time for activities that you love to do.

Positive feeling 1-10	Time spent doing them last week	Activity	Time you plan to spend on them next week.

From your earlier list and using the list above, what things can you easily add into your daily schedule?

Notice how minor adjustments in your life can really have an impact.

Start NOW!

You now have a real package of happiness boosters to put in your life. Why not decide now to have a daily happiness and pleasure habit? Fear and worry are great at separating us from feeling good; conversely, feeling good dissipates worry and fear.

Spontaneous giving, showing gratitude and kindness to others, even in the smallest of ways, boost happiness. Eating chocolate or ice cream is a great pleasure booster; the positive feeling is brief but when savoured it becomes a lasting positive memory. Appreciating what you have, being with other people and developing skills you love are all ways to increase your happiness.

When we do things that bring us positive emotion, we are inclined to continue and repeat the experience. Feeling good can be both momentary pleasure and pleasure as a reward. Positive feeling is made from our responses to present experiences, and our ability to draw positive emotions from past experience.

 **brilliant** recap

This chapter is full of ways to get more positive emotion in your life. Remember:

- Every time you experience happiness and positive feelings and emotion, this becomes a memory from which you can draw and repeat.

- Be open and curious. Every time you learn a new skill or push yourself to do something that gives a positive feeling, you get a boost that invigorates you to try again.

- Be grateful for what you have and you'll enjoy more.

- Be kind if you want to be happier.

- Be with other people.

- Be yourself.

- Variety is the spice of life: when you do new things you build up resources and happiness.

- Increase your opportunities for flow by becoming more engaged, focused and challenged. When we are lost to an activity for its own sake we feel great.

- Remember to stop and savour. Take pleasure in your senses and the joy of 'now'.

In the next chapter we'll look at building on this, using what we do best to achieve goals that will help make us happier and more fulfilled.

CHAPTER 4

Do more of what you love and set better goals

Go confident in the direction of your dreams. Live the life you've imagined. Our aspirations are our possibilities

Samuel Johnson 1705–84

Do you get up in the morning excited about the day?

Having a goal and a direction in life is fundamental to psychological well-being; having goals that enable us to develop our strengths is even better. We have seen in the last chapter that being engaged and challenged in life is essential to well-being. This chapter is going to focus on what you need in order to start setting great goals and doing more things that are congruent with who you are. We'll look again at positive emotion and how it is key to much more than just feeling good (the fuel in the tank that generates interest, motivation and engagement) and how this can be used to build motivation and action into your life.

Natural talent

Research shows that not only is it important for your well-being to have goals, but that you are more likely to achieve your goals when they reflect and utilise what you naturally want to do and have a talent for. Have you noticed that some things are easy while other things remain on the to-do list interminably? As we touched on in the last chapter, when you are intrinsically motivated you don't need reward; the reward is the activity itself. Knowing what is going on when you are doing things you love and understanding this better can help you to get more excitement and challenge into your life by setting goals that you really **want** to achieve.

Being authentic

When somebody is 'in their skin', they are recognised for being good at what they are doing as if they were born to be that way. Mick Jagger on stage **is** Mick Jagger, and anybody else is just a poor imitation. Being authentic, like beauty, is hard to define but is easily recognisable. We respond to people who are good at what they do when it appears as second nature, when they look unforced, expert and confident. Authentic people hold the quality of having purpose and action in harmony and there is an honesty of natural ability that engenders confidence and respect.

Remembering flow

Imagine using the same ingredients that lead to flow experiences to energise you to meet your goals. Being in flow uses skills that are easy to recognise, such as playing an instrument, playing a sport, or being creative. But flow experiences also include personal characteristics that are meaningful to us. Look back at the things you noted down as activities that offer opportunities for you to be in flow from the last chapter; are there any activities that you love because you get to be the best that you are?

Finding your strengths

What aspects of your character do you most value and love using? For example, are you 'you' when you are funny, kind, responsible, reliable, loving, passionate, forgiving etc? Write down and remember what character strengths you most identify with:

The 'father' of positive psychology, Martin Seligman, believes we can only really flourish when we are using our signature character strengths. According to Seligman, you are using a character strength when:

- It feels authentic and gives you a sense of your real self.
- You feel excited.
- There is and has been a rapid learning curve involved.
- It offers new ways to use existing skills.
- You yearn to do/be this.
- There is an inevitability about doing this and you feel unable to stop yourself from doing it.
- You feel invigorated rather than depleted doing this.
- You find yourself engaging in activities and projects that require you to be this way.
- You feel joy and enthusiasm.[63]

Signature strengths

When we are behaving in a way that meets the criteria above, Martin Seligman believes we are using our 'signature character strengths'. For Seligman there are 24 universal character strengths. A strength is defined in two ways: first as 'a trait', an underlying psychological characteristic, and secondly as something valued in its own right, desired as a quality for nothing but itself. He and fellow positive psychologist Christopher Peterson spent a long time examining criteria considered to be character strengths from across history and nations, and all the strengths are expressions of six core human characteristics or 'virtues:

- Wisdom and knowledge
- Courage
- Love and humanity
- Justice

- Temperance
- Spirituality and transcendence.[64]

---

brilliant exercise

Why not take 20 minutes now to find your signature strengths at www. authentichappiness.com, VIA (values in action) signature strengths questionnaire, or look at the following list and give a number from 1 to 10 to each as to how much you use this strength, how much it shows up in your life and then how much you would like it to.

Values in action – signature character strengths	How much is this in your life?	How much would you like this to be in your life?
1 Curiosity and interest in the world		
2 Love of learning		
3 Judgement/critical thinking/open-mindedness		
4 Ingenuity/originality/practical intelligence/ street smart		
5 Social/personal/emotional intelligence		
6 Perspective		
7 Valour and bravery		
8 Perseverance/industry/diligence		
9 Integrity/genuineness/honesty		
10 Kindness and generosity		
11 Loving and allowing oneself to be loved		
12 Citizenship/duty/teamwork/loyalty		
13 Fairness and equity		
14 Leadership		

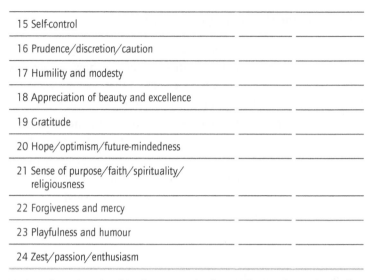

15 Self-control		
16 Prudence/discretion/caution		
17 Humility and modesty		
18 Appreciation of beauty and excellence		
19 Gratitude		
20 Hope/optimism/future-mindedness		
21 Sense of purpose/faith/spirituality/ religiousness		
22 Forgiveness and mercy		
23 Playfulness and humour		
24 Zest/passion/enthusiasm		

Notice where there is a big discrepancy in the numbers and remake the list in priority order. You will find that most of these strengths show up in some part of your life; the important thing to notice is which strengths are easier and more natural.

When you are using your strengths you are much more likely to be engaged in what you are doing. When you are engaged, you are energised and enjoy what you are doing. Using your strengths is therefore a brilliant way to be motivated and achieve your goals.

 insight

Research has shown that people who use their strengths to achieve their goals are more likely to achieve them as well as feel more fulfilled and happy with goals that use strengths.[65]

Using strengths to express values

Strengths are the psychological characteristics through which we honour and express what we **value** in our life; how we actively integrate who we are with what we value. Often we love a *context* because we have the opportunity to engage in, and use our strengths in support of, what we value. If for instance the emotional need or value is to show courage, the 'context' in which we find this need or value can vary. In the case of courage it might be mountaineering, joining the army, performing or being an entrepreneur. No matter the context, we will **flourish** if it provides the opportunity to use our character strengths.

 **example**

Here is an example of how different character strengths can meet the same value. All the following people love risk or adventure in their lives because they value courage, and are happy when they are meeting this need because the character strengths they use when facing adventure and risk are natural to them.

- When facing risk and adventure a mountaineer gets the chance to be brave, curious, ingenious, show perseverance or self-control.

- A soldier can show valour, leadership, teamwork, loyalty or courage.

- The performer can also show courage, enthusiasm, passion or self-control.

- The entrepreneur can use courage, originality, optimism, enthusiasm, creative thinking or diligence.

All of the above characters love to be courageous but do so in different ways. They all need risk and adventure but the way in which they express courage can vary widely in activity and context because they hold different character strengths and talents.

We **love** to use our strengths; they are not skills any more than courage is a skill. The character strength is how we express what we value and need emotionally in our life: 'values in action' (Seligman's 'VIA') are at the heart of most of our intrinsic goals.

What do we mean by values?

Values are the way we prioritise what we **need**; they are learned rather than innate. What we give most value to governs the choices we make. Values guide both our choices and actions. They are how we prioritise needs that govern what we value and make us different from each other. We can become blocked when one value clashes with another, because it indicates a clash of needs. Your values reflect your emotional needs and noticing the strength of feeling you give to a value, or the response you feel when a value is threatened, can indicate a priority need. Most values are easily identified, such as honesty, respect, trust, integrity, love or courage. We will look much further at the connection of needs to what we value in Chapter 7. However, it is important to know what you value and need when thinking about setting goals, because the goals you are most likely to achieve will be those that are congruent with what you value and which allow you an opportunity to use your natural character strengths.

Your values therefore effect and prioritise your choices and goals; without a hierarchy of needs we could not make choices.

Can you think what might be your top five 'values'? What can you not live without? If you answer family, what values are represented in family life that meet your most important needs? Another way to find your values is to notice what you most hate and cannot bear to be around; your values are missing or threatened in this circumstance. Chapter 7 goes into this more fully.

Finding what we value is important because it gives us a context within which we can use our strengths. **When we are 'in our skin,' our strengths AND what we value are in harmony.**

The words and meanings can get in the way when some concepts are interchangeable. Love is a value to many people as it is something they can't live without and love can also be the activity as well as the characteristic signature strength that honours the value. However, love can also be expressed through gratitude, forgiveness, courage, loyalty, passion, kindness, integrity, etc.

Not all positive psychologists working with strengths are doing so from such a value-laden perspective. The Clifton strength-finder[66] holds a much longer list of strengths that are more slanted towards business 'skills'. And at www.cappeu.com, the Centre for Applied Positive Psychology,[67] you can take a very comprehensive test for a small fee. This is a great tool as it is less hierarchical than Seligman's VIA and allows you to hold many top strengths, as well as highlighting the strengths you don't use enough and those you could pay more attention to.

brilliant exercise

Stop for a minute and list your five top strengths:

For each of the following areas of life in the table below, list a positive moment or activity and the character strength you were using at the time.

Then think of a goal (small or large) that you would like to achieve in each area, and describe the strengths you will use to achieve it.

Area of life	Good moment/ positive activity	Character strength	Goal	Character strength
At work				
With family				
In your living environment				

With friends				
With significant other				
When having fun				
Looking after your health				
Personal growth/ learning				
Economically				
Spiritually/the wider world				

- Notice any part of your life that could do with some attention and try to think of an imaginative way to use your strengths in that area.

- Notice if you are not using one of your top strengths.

- Can you think of a new way of using your top strengths to support or change something in your life for the better?

- Decide to do three things this week in different areas of your life that will excite you.

brilliant insight

Remember variety – using your signature strengths in a **new** way has a lasting effect on increasing happiness and reducing symptoms of depression.[68]

Why not list your strengths in the first column of the following table and think of new ways of using them in different areas of your life.

Top character strengths	Area of life	Area of life	Area of life
1 e.g. kindness			
2			

Top character strengths	Area of life	Area of life	Area of life
3			
4			
5			

Three importants points to remember about using your strengths

1 Use your top character strengths

If you are not using your signature strengths enough you will not feel as good as when you do! Find new ways to use your strengths; try using your strengths in all areas of your life. If your top strength is critical thinking, judgement or open-mindedness, do you apply this strength to your emotional life as much as your working life?

2 Notice and pay attention to those character traits at the bottom of your list!

Using only your top strengths, indulging your passions, can lead to neglecting what is hard. If kindness and generosity are at the bottom of your list and creativity and love of learning at the top, try using your top strengths to develop those at the bottom. Start to get creative about being kind, or if you have a top strength that is bravery and valour – dare to be kind! Sarah found that the worst part of her day was walking home from work in the dark – bravery was at the bottom of her list. By using creativity, her top strength, she thought up different ways to go home and creative tasks to fulfil on the way home to distract her from her apprehension and it has now become a fulfilling part of her day and she is much braver as a consequence.

3 Beware of becoming one dimensional

It is also worth noting that an overdeveloped strength can be a weakness. Being overly preoccupied with the strengths you are good at can get out of balance. Too much kindness, an overly developed sense of fairness or too much self-control is not healthy and can prevent you flourishing as much as not using your top strengths. A truly flourishing life is one that contains many strengths.

Now that you have a clearer idea of what you care about and what you are best at, how can your strengths and values become part of your goals?

Goals

What are goals? Goals are anything we set ourselves to do. All human action is to some extent goal directed, from getting up in the morning and going to work, to running a marathon, writing a letter or being a good parent. A goal is anything we wish to get done either in the short term or over a lifetime. Goals are also how we meet our most basic needs.

Your actions and goals respond to your most basic needs

We looked at the six basic needs that psychologist Carol Ryff believes are essential to our psychological well-being in Chapter 2 and research by other psychologists[69] has found the following four basic needs to be the most satisfying to us when they are met.

1 **Self-esteem**. Liking yourself and feeling good about who you are and your abilities. Goals that build your self-esteem will be the most satisfying to you.

2 **Competence. Able to function in your environment (environmental mastery).** You need to have the skills and ability to achieve what you want – you need *competence*.

Your competence includes all your physical and cognitive skills; your goals are affected by your ability to problem solve as well as having or getting the skills required.

3 **Relatedness – you need to feel connected to others (positive relations with others).** We want and need to be accepted. Goals that are connected to your relatedness to others are those that bring you closer to other people and bring you the satisfaction of feeling loved and cared about.

4 **Self-directed. We need to be ourselves (autonomy).** Finally there are self-directed tasks and goals, those actions you are free to choose for yourself, the tasks you enjoy for their own sake, and would do without obligation or direction. We do these things just because we want to and enjoy doing so. These are mostly intrinsically motivated actions; we are self-directed and *autonomous*. You are much more likely to achieve the goals in this category because they are more likely to be intrinsically motivated.

⤤ brilliant insight

Autonomy and being intrinsically motivated are fantastic for achieving your goals, not just because you feel more pleasure and engagement when you are doing something you love to do but also because you are more creative and better at problem solving when you are intrinsically motivated.[70] Remember over-justification from Chapter 2: being given outside incentives to problem solve reduces your pleasure in the task as well as your ability.

Being creative is an emotionally driven process; the happier you are, the more creative you become. This is not to dispute the widespread belief in the tortured miserable artist, and this book cannot begin to address that debate. The psychologist Dean Simonton differentiates between 'small c' creativity that enhances everyday life and problem-solving skills and 'big C' creativity that makes lasting contributions to culture and history,[71] and for this chapter we only need 'small c' creativity to flourish.

Fulfilling our needs is at the heart of all we do and the more important the basic need, the better we feel when we are doing things that feed that need. These four basic needs have been consistently shown to be what satisfy us most when they are met.

Research has shown that of a further six needs – self-actualisation, physical thriving/health, security, pleasure, money, poularity/influence – making money is the least satisfying.[72]

brilliant tip

Self-determination theory holds that competence, relatedness and autonomy are the three most basic and essential human needs.[73]

brilliant definition

Goals that are self-determined:

- Involve doing things you are good at and using your strengths
- Challenge you and allow you to improve and learn new skills that you enjoy
- Have no form of reward, no extrinsic pressure except that the task or activity is undertaken for its own sake
- Involve other people where you feel supported and connected.

Have a purpose that is part of a larger agenda that is important to you. Tasks and activities are congruent to what matters to you – a new habit that holds a purpose, training for an adventure or sports challenge you really want to achieve, dieting because you value your health, etc., or are part of something you want, such as working towards an exam or promotion. (Doing any of these things because a parent or partner wants it is not self-determined.)

Uncertainty

Having goals and direction is an important ingredient of well-being and life satisfaction. However, goals must be achievable without being certain. A level of uncertainty provides challenge and demands *hope*. We need both to believe we **can** do it and then to be **committed** to doing so.

Hope

Positive psychologist C.R. Snyder believes that hope is much more than a passive emotion, containing two ingredients that together give us the mental and emotional capacity essential to reaching our goals: **ability** and **energy**. Hopeful thinking involves: the *ability to problem solve* – the mental ability to solve and devise ways to achieve a goal; and the *energy to carry out the plan* – the motivational force to carry these thoughts through with action.[74]

Positive thinking is better thinking

An important discovery supported by a variety of research is that 'looking on the bright side' and being positive about life enables better thinking. It has been shown that people who are hopeful and optimistic in outlook are more likely to be able to think more clearly and rationally than those who look for the worst to happen. We have looked at the effect on our cognitive ability that *feeling* positive can have. Positive psychology is clearly demonstrating that *thinking* positively also affects our rational ability. Chapter 6, which deals with optimism, will look at this further, but start with the idea that you **can** and **will** achieve the goals you set yourself. Starting to think this way will get your brain in action.

 They are able who think they are able.

Virgil 70–19 BC Roman poet

brilliant definition

The ability to see clearly what the goals are and to be able to work out how we are going to get there. This is called *pathways* thinking.

To be able to initiate the action, generate and sustain the confidence and motivation to carry out the plan – 'travel the pathway'. This is called *agency* thinking.

Hopeful thinking = pathways + agency[75]

Hopeful thinking is the combination of both a plan and the energy and confidence to carry it out.

The plan (the pathway) is ruled by your reason.

brilliant tip

Things that help you think better:

● Positive emotion

● Intrinsic motivation

● Growth mindset

The action (the agency) is ruled by your emotion and passion.

brilliant tip

Things that motivate you to action:

● Using your strengths

● Fulfilling your needs and values

Your emotion is governed by your individual needs, values and desires. We are already some way to understanding this side of us better, and will deal even more with the power and potential of our emotions in the next chapter.

The psychologist Jonathan Haidt in his book, *The Happiness Hypothesis*, uses the analogy of a rider on an elephant. The elephant is our passion and desires, which, untamed, has the strength to go where it will. Our will, our mind, is the rider on the elephant and is not nearly as strong.[76] When we remember the strength of the elephant it makes much more sense to understand and work with him rather than try to do battle. The elephant holds our values and core beliefs and is the energy that carries us. Knowing better what we really desire and need in our lives is reflected in our passions and enthusiasms (what we need and value). Our needs and desires, our true nature, are the elephant. The rider is our reason, our problem-solving, cognitive ability; it can guide and control the elephant, but if the needs and desires of the elephant are in conflict with the rider the elephant gets his way. Understanding what really motivates you starts by examining your core needs and beliefs. Using your strengths is like having control of your elephant.

Emotional feedback

When we achieve our goals we feel great and it is in this way that being hopeful is an emotional process. This emotion is important, as it is fed back into future goal-directed thinking. When we fail we feel bad and the negative emotion contributes to unhopeful future goal direction. This emotional part of the process is why it is important to look at and better understand which goals we are choosing, what values and needs our goals contain and will deliver to us, and what past experience is reflected in how hopeful we are of succeeding.

 **exercise**

Finding what makes us hopeful

Your past is a great way to start thinking about what makes you hopeful. If you have succeeded or failed, understand what it was that drove you to success and what causes you to give up.

Think of a past successful goal

- Why did you want to do this?
- What were the biggest problems?
- What solutions did you find to problems or barriers?
- What motivated you initially?
- What kept you motivated?
- What strengths did you use most?
- How did you feel at the beginning/middle/end?
- What did you learn?

Take a moment to think about a goal you would really like to achieve and write clearly what it is.

Now answer the following questions with a score between 1 and 10.

- How much do you want to achieve this?
- How motivated are you?
- How excited are you by the challenge?
- How much confidence will achieving this goal give you?
- How much support do you have?
- How much do your skills match the challenge?
- How much is this goal a reflection of what you really value and care about?
- How much is this your goal, *your* choice?

These questions are for your interest. Have any of your answers made you question your choice? If the goal is hard and a real challenge but you are motivated and excited, the following questions will start to put some practical thinking and motivation in place.

Positive steps to achieving your goals

- Write down clearly why you want to achieve this goal.
- Name the value it fulfils and any conflicting values that achieving this will affect. Do you need to choose one over the other?
- Name the character strengths that you can use to help achieve it.
- What is your belief in the outcome and how realistic are the beliefs you hold that are important to achieving this goal? (We will look at this more closely in Chapter 6.)
- How can you be more positive, using past experience of success?
- What will it mean to you to achieve this goal?
- How can you enjoy the process as much as the result? What will be fun or exciting?
- What are the practical issues?
- Can you break your goal down into smaller challenges or mini-goals? What is the first step?
- Can you be more creative in your approach?
- Where can you get the support you need? Do you need someone to help you?
- Is there a skill you need to learn first?
- Are you using a growth mindset? How can you create opportunities that will support your goal?

As you think about these questions, notice when you are excited and when you are daunted. Try to understand what it is that is giving you positive energy and move towards using those avenues and try to think creatively as to how you can increase those qualities and aspects that match your strengths.

brilliant tip

Why not use positive psychologist Shane Lopez's GPOWER?

G – what is the GOAL?

P – What is the stated PATHWAY?

O – What OBSTACLES are in the pathway?

W – What is the source of WILLPOWER that will energise you?

E – Which pathway did you finally ELECT to follow?

R – RETHINK the process. Would you do it the same way if you did it again?[77]

Past experiences and their influence on your goals

With any goal you can have many great strategies for achieving it, for example as getting a new job, you know that you could network as much as you can, get a qualification or training, update your CV, and keep up to date on what's out there in the advertised section of the papers. If the weeks and months are going by and it is still only a plan, what is stopping you putting this plan into action? Was it because the last few times you applied for a job you didn't even get an interview? Are there issues such as if you got a new job you might have to move house and the last time you moved it was painful and you still miss your friends? Or is it that every time you try something new you somehow end up worse off? The problem is in the past experience. If the emotional energy connected to such a goal is negative it is hardly surprising that however much the goal is desired, the initiative and motivation to move to action are blocked. We will look at how this can be changed in more detail in Chapter 6. Changing the plan and remembering what has worked in the past, reframing the strategy in a way that reflects past success if only in the smallest steps, are a way to unblocking and moving forward.

Is action in conflict with your values?

Sometimes people get stuck when there is a clash of values, such as pursuing a career and fulfilling your work potential at the cost of your need to fulfil your nurturing generous self that is fulfilled in family life. Examples of other value conflicts could be the need for both certainty and safety vs risk and courage; duty vs fairness. If you are having trouble achieving something you want and you can't quite get going, it may be a clash of values.

Goals and fear

One of the most common reasons people don't achieve their goals is fear. As we have already mentioned, fear can be connected to past experience but most fear is irrational. Building your positive emotion is a great way to dissipate fear. Break goals down into manageable chunks and remember that sometimes it can also be success we are afraid of. Building a growth mindset that is interested in learning through the process of aiming for something, is a great way to build your confidence and skills. Pay attention to your elephant, let your passions shine and you will increase your self-belief as well as your well-being. Remember, feeling good is the best way to drown out negative thinking!

Improving self-efficacy or self-belief

 Self efficacy is the belief in one's capabilities to organise and execute the sources of action required to manage prospective situations.

Albert Bandura, 1986

Self-efficacy is a huge subject in psychology; literally thousands of articles have been written and countless research studies have been conducted into why, if we believe we can do something, we are more likely to succeed. Self-efficacy is very important to how motivated we feel; if we believe we *can* achieve a goal we are more likely to want to do it. Psychologist James Maddux defines self-efficacy as 'what I believe I can do with my skills under certain conditions'.[78] It is a belief in both personal skills *and* the ability to use them, **not** as a wish or will to do so, but as a confident *can*. The psychologist Albert Bandura introduced the concept of self-efficacy in 1977 and tells us that self-efficacy comes mainly from our own experience but that it can also be vicarious.[79] Seeing someone else do something encourages us to believe that we can do the same, and other people's belief and encouragement can also affect our own belief in achieving our goal. Bandura also talks of the effect our mood has on what we choose to do and our ability to regulate and use our emotions as a motivating factor.

Your self-efficacy influences your choices because the more you believe in yourself, the more choices you have. It gives you the ability to be self-reflective in a way that positively affects the choices you make. This in turn affects your competencies, inter-ests and social networks which contribute to and determine your life course.

↗ **brilliant** impact

Ways to strengthen and develop self-efficacy:

- Expand your experience. Try new things.
- Set achievable goals that build both confidence and an experience of success.
- Use your imagination – imagine doing or having done something.
- Look to people you admire and would like to imitate, especially people who have achieved goals you would like to attain. If they can do it, so can you!
- Using and understanding your emotions – the next chapter will cover this.
- Seeking the support and encouragement of others.

brilliant tip

The higher your self-efficacy, the better choices you make!

Self-efficacy affects your motivation, how you feel about yourself, how much you persevere, your health, and the things you choose to do.

As a coach I get my clients to visualise, as realistically as possible, doing something, and imagining the emotions and effect of succeeding: literally to 'try on' the experience. There is no doubt that believing you can do something works.

brilliant goals

- Support and reflect your values
- Involve using your strengths

- Offer the chance to be in flow
- Are autonomous, they are *your* choice
- You are committed to achieving
- You are competent, you have the necessary ability and skills
- You enjoy and are excited by them
- Are part of a bigger purpose
- Open up opportunities
- Have clear steps
- Build your self-belief

brilliant tip

- Celebrate small achievements along the way.
- Let go of what doesn't work and move on. All experience counts, and no one gets anywhere without having some failure.
- Laugh at yourself if it doesn't work.
- Don't let negative voices get too loud.
- Don't engage in self-pity, blame or ruminate over what isn't working.
- Don't constantly evaluate how you are doing.

brilliant exercise

- Decide on which goal from your table you will achieve this week.
- Tell a friend you are going to do it.
- Celebrate with this friend when you have done it.

 recap

- This chapter has introduced you to the idea of how using your strengths affects both your well-being and your ability to achieve your goals in different areas of your life.

- You have thought about what you value and started to notice when your goals reflect and feed your values and when they don't.

- We have started to examine how our basic needs can govern our goal direction.

- We have looked at how being self-directed and intrinsically motivated is a vital motivating force.

- We have looked at the two important factors necessary to achieving your goals: problem solving and motivation to action. We have thought about what supports both these factors and makes you more hopeful.

- We have seen that belief in ourselves is an important ingredient in achieving what we want.

- Finally, you have chosen one great goal that you are committed to achieving.

- I hope also that you are feeling more confident in yourself and excited about setting new goals that will give you a challenge you will enjoy. The next chapter will examine how you can understand and use your emotions better, not just to improve your relationships but in all areas of your life.

CHAPTER 5

Emotional well-being: Building better relationships with ourselves and others

The world is a looking-glass and gives back to every man the reflection of his own face.

William Makepeace Thackeray, 1811–63

In Chapter 3 we looked at the importance of positive emotions and the effect that feeling good has on our physical and mental well-being. We saw how this works as a feedback loop that is essential to our ability to grow and develop in all areas of our lives. This chapter, although concerned with the subject of our *emotional* well-being, is all about how we *think*, with and about, our emotions. Emotions inform and drive us in every area of our lives; the more we understand ourselves emotionally, the more able we are to understand other people and respond and act *with* our emotions and desires rather than at their mercy. We can 'think' better when *informed* by our emotions rather than in conflict with them.

We will cover the importance of emotional intelligence: how you understand, use and manage your emotions, and how you can have better relationships when you take time to understand a little better what you and other people are feeling, and why. Remember the rider and the elephant: sometimes we are so busy judging and examining other elephants and riders we forget that we ourselves are sitting on an equally wilful beast.

 **tip**

Having good relationships with others is affected by how good a relationship we have with ourselves. Having a good relationship with ourselves involves having a good mental relationship with our emotions.

Emotional control

The conflict between emotion and reason is a deeply held idea and is the duality within Greek philosophy and most religions, subjugating base desire to the service of higher rational thinking. In fact, it is so ingrained that most cultures see unregulated emotion as socially taboo; in some cultures expressing *any* emotion (not just unregulated emotion) is seen as weakness. Being able to control our emotions is a basic requirement of social acceptance and display of adult maturity. The connection of our desires to our thoughts is mostly understood in this way; as the subservience of passion to reason. This attitude to emotion can keep us in emotional ignorance. Emotional intelligence redresses the balance, and research is encouraging us to recognise our emotions as a vital tool, as intelligent as our minds. Our emotions are integral to thinking. Just as we use our thinking to inform and regulate our feelings, so understanding and utilising our feelings and emotions inform and contribute to our intelligence. We think *with* our emotions as well as *about* our emotions.

Flourishing emotionally, feeling supported, understood, connected and related, are such a fundamental human need that it is surprising that learning emotional intelligence is mostly left to us to figure out for ourselves and build on emotional knowledge learned from relationships formed in infancy. The relationship you had with your mother will have an effect on all your relationships.

Emotional intelligence

In the past, pure logical 'mental' intelligence has explained why some people do better in life. IQ was the only measurable indicator of ability and success. The psychologist Howard Gardner was one of the first to speak of multi-intelligences.[80] He believed that we use at least eight competencies in how we function both internally (within ourselves) and with other people (interpersonally). *Emotional* intelligence (EQ) is our social and communication skills.

What is EQ?

Some psychologists working in the field of emotional intelligence, such as Daniel Goleman and Richard Boyatzis, believe emotional intelligence to be clusters of competencies; a person can be described as emotionally intelligent when they show 'the competencies that constitute self awareness, self management, social awareness and social skills at appropriate times and ways in sufficient frequency to be effective in the situation'.[81] Positive psychologist Rueven Bar-On measures emotional intelligence as an even more comprehensive combination of emotional abilities; he believes that there are at least ten contributing factors to emotional and social intelligence.

brilliant tip

Contributing factors to emotional and social intelligence:

- Self-regard, accurate self-appraisal, inner strength
- Interpersonal relationships, social responsibility, wanting relationships and at ease with others
- Impulse control, can control aggression
- Problem solving
- Emotional self-awareness
- Flexibility, able to adapt and change
- Reality testing – able to assess emotions accurately
- Stress tolerance, understanding and controlling one's mood, able to handle and affect environment or events
- Assertiveness, able to express oneself
- Empathy, warmth towards others.[82]

How many of Rueven Bar-On's emotional skills do you think you are good at and use?

Measuring EQ

It is now increasingly accepted that emotional intelligence (EQ) can be assessed and measured, just as IQ can be assessed, and that scoring well in this ability indicates your potential to succeed, not just socially, but in every area of your life. It is now believed by many people to be a more significant indicator of ability than IQ.

Any measurement that segregates ability has the potential to harm someone; however, acknowledging that social skills and our ability to function emotionally are vital skills that can be improved and learned by deeper understanding can only be a good thing. We should and can engage better with our emotions, and see them as more than mere helpless and passionate responses or the vagaries of personality type.

John Mayer, Peter Salovey and David Caruso, positive psychologists working in the forefront of emotional intelligence, use an ability-based measure[83] that breaks emotional intelligence into four separate skills: perceiving emotions, using emotions, understanding emotions and managing emotions. They believe that each of these ways of showing emotional intelligence can be measured and together can assess someone's emotional skills.[84] We can look at emotional intelligence through these four skills.

1 Perceiving emotions
We perceive emotions in other people by recognising their facial and physical expressions.

---

brilliant insight

Emotional facial expressions are the same throughout the world. The only differences are in what emotions are acceptable to display; these can be gender and culturally influenced.[85]

Being good at *perceiving* emotions means being able to:

- Know your own emotions
- Recognise emotions in another person's facial expression
- Recognise emotions in objects and art
- Express emotions appropriately
- See when someone is showing false emotion.

⟋ brilliant insight

When researching facial expression, psychologist Paul Eckman found that after pulling faces all day to understand in detail the different muscle combinations used to express subtly different emotions, he actually 'felt' the emotions he had pulled a face to represent. This has been shown to be true with research that controlled facial expressions and discovered that expressions give rise to the emotion as well as the emotion giving rise to the expression. This is called the 'facial feedback' hypothesis. The movements of face muscles actually affect the emotional experience.[86] A great piece of research that proved this was when people were either prevented from smiling or encouraged to smile by having to hold a pencil in their mouths. Those who held a pencil in their teeth and couldn't smile properly rated cartoons less funny than did those who didn't have a pencil in their mouths.[87]

Research has proved that if you smile you will feel better. Try it: see if pulling an angry face starts to make you feel that way. Or smile and the world might get brighter.

Your posture also has an effect on your emotion; try feeling kind with your hands on your hips compared with a relaxed posture.

 **exercise**

How many emotions can you remember feeling and what caused you to feel this or that way?

Affection, love, attraction, compassion, sentiment, desire, infatuation, longing, amusement, delight, satisfaction, elation, joy, excitement, thrill, enthusiasm, contentment, pleasure, pride, hope, relief, surprise, amazement, irritation, annoyance, frustration, anger, hostility, resentment, bitterness, spite, disgust, hate, contempt, envy, jealousy, hurt, anguish, depression, grief, sorrow, misery, disappointment, remorse, guilt, shame, isolation, insult, insecurity, embarrassment, humiliation, defeat, neglect, reflection, sympathy, pity, empathy, tenderness, fear, horror, panic, nervousness, dread, distress, apprehension, tenseness, stress, longing, passion.

- What emotions are you feeling about yourself at this moment?
- How loving and kind do you feel towards yourself at this moment?
- What feelings are helpful and what feelings are getting in the way?
- Think of a time or incident when it was important to identify either your own or someone else's emotions.

Taking time to think about these questions will get you thinking about emotions. Notice if you are limiting yourself to general happy/sad feelings or if you can be more nuanced and subtle. Try to broaden your awareness and perception to be more precise and inclusive.

2 Using emotions

Our emotions help us to think. Positive emotions literally help us think better and more creatively.

 **example**

Research by psychologist Alice Isen found that doctors were more likely to diagnose well and interact and learn more from the patient when their natural mood state was lifted, than when they were not.[88]

Emotions impact every thought and decision you make. Your emotions even affect your memory as well as your ability to function.

 **insight**

Research has shown that our mood affects our memory. When in a negative or neutral mood we are more likely to be able to recall bad memories, and when we are in a happy or positive mood it is easier to remember good things.[89]

brilliant tip

Lift your mood for the task in hand

- Keep a cool head when processing detailed or accurate work.
- Encourage a positive atmosphere and mood for thinking creatively and in new ways.
- Understand that the mood we are in supports and affects our cognitive ability.

3 Understanding emotions

Emotions progress over time and are complex. Understanding emotions well includes recognition of this complexity in other people, insight into why people feel the way they do, and knowledge that they will not always feel this way. *Understanding* why someone feels the way they do makes it possible to project into the future ideas about how things might be. Understanding the complexity of our own feelings allows us to interpret others' responses in a more measured way. People who are good at understanding emotions are the sort of people who, when you are with them, make you feel that they 'get you'. It is a very empathetic skill that can also be called insightful.

Emotions are not one-dimensional; it is possible to feel more than one emotion at a time. Emotional psychologist Robert Plutchik says that there are eight basic emotions, and eight advanced emotions that are composed of two of the basic emotions.[90] The basic emotions also sit within a sliding scale of intensity. All other

Rage	**Anger**	Annoyance
	Aggression	
Vigilance	**Anticipation**	Interest
	Optimism	
Ecstasy	**Joy**	Serenity
	Love	
Admiration	**Trust**	Acceptance
	Submission	
Terror	**Fear**	Apprehension
	Awe	
Amazement	**Surprise**	Distraction
	Disappointment	
Grief	**Sadness**	Pensiveness
	Remorse	
Loathing	**Disgust**	Boredom
	Contempt	
Rage	**Anger**	Annoyance

Figure 5.1 Robert Plutchik's basic and advanced emotions

emotions, for Plutchik, are a combination of any of the basic emotions or similar and on the sliding scale (Figure 5.1).

Understanding that emotions are complicated and that many can be felt simultaneously requires attention. Emotions are closely linked to what you value, to past experiences and to your needs. The feelings you have are within you and about you. Emotions are what shape both your story and the way you respond. You may have emotional issues that stem from your desires and needs, especially if these needs are not being met or they are under attack.

If you are not dealing with an emotional issue that is causing conflict and pain within you, you may respond very strongly to behaviour or need in someone else who reflects this emotion. You will notice it more and almost seek it out; you can even imagine it is there in order to attack it. You can recognise this if you have ever reacted strongly to someone in a negative way. What were they doing or saying? Were they attacking one of your values? Were they displaying something about yourself you are unhappy with?

We can become better at noticing our emotional responses. We can stop and check if something might have triggered us to react in some particular way; or perhaps someone else is projecting their issues onto us – this can be the case if you feel attacked for no reason. This is sometimes called 'mirroring' because the emotion is responding to the mirror of itself. There is a brilliant example of this in the film *Mona Lisa* where a girl at the receiving end of an emotional attack knows it to be her attacker's issue and simply steps forward and holds her in an embrace rather than attacking back. In the story the girl being attacked had knowledge of her attacker's issue; this, of course, is not always the case in day-to-day exchanges. It is very powerful to notice properly the emotions in others and question why someone might be feeling the way they do. Anger can be the public expression of pain, anxiety, fear, jealousy or grief.

 **tip**

Next time you see someone who appears angry, stop for a minute to ask yourself if they may be anxious, afraid or unhappy for some reason. Aggression is a very good indicator of fear.

Feeling anxious can make you appear and look angry and this first impression can never be redeemed. This is not advice to 'fake it to make it' but to be aware of the complexity of emotions within us, and how they are expressed and perceived.

4 Managing emotions

This is a longer-term strategy; managing emotions is how you bring about the best emotional outcome. This basically means believing that you can do something to make yourself feel better in stressful or upsetting circumstances. (There is more on how to do this in the next chapter.) Being good at managing emotions involves being able to make long-term strategies that are both active and directed at the problem – deciding what to do and doing it.

 **tip**

People who are good at managing emotions are able to:
- Stay open to their feelings
- Regulate their mood when necessary
- Understand the role emotions are playing in themselves and others
- Handle the emotion in situations, in other people, and themselves
- Employ strategies to change moods and emotions
- Assess and learn from the effectiveness of these strategies.

↗ brilliant insight

Noticing how we are feeling and the emotions in others is a skill that varies; some people are naturally good at it. Autism and Asperger's sufferers are not very good at reading emotion but they can be taught.

Catching your feelings

Whatever the situation, you can stop and assess your emotions. Stopping and counting to ten is a great way to give yourself space to notice what you are feeling or to become aware of what someone else is feeling. Catching your emotions before they catch you is a great way to give yourself time to modify or change your mood. Notice physical warnings such a tightness in the stomach.

Good ways to manage your emotions in the short term are:

- Exercise, go for a walk
- Listen to music
- Social support, turn to a friend
- Relax.

Longer-term strategies for managing your emotions involve both action and direction, engaging with the problem and having a plan. Hopeful thinking is good for long-term emotional management.

Bad strategies for managing your emotions in the short or long term are:

- Alcohol
- Procrastination
- Overeating
- Oversleeping.

In the next chapter we will look at good emotional coping strategies in more detail.

Mostly we recognise and respond to emotions subconsciously. Remembering, or being present enough, to take account of the fact that what you are feeling is affecting how you are thinking is good emotional management.

In an ideal world we would all become as emotionally steady as the Dalai Lama. Learning to accept, understand and manage how we are feeling takes time and practice, even when we are lucky enough to be born innately empathetic and emotionally skilled.

Putting emotional intelligence to work

- Do you respond badly to certain emotions in others?
- Or in yourself?
- How do you want other people to feel when they are with you?
- Do you feel this way yourself?

 exercise

Becoming aware of your emotional intelligence:

- Describe a situation that occurred in the last month, in which you successfully identified and managed your own emotions and those of others.

- What skills did you use to manage your emotions? And those of other people?

- Describe a situation in which it was critical for you to identify and manage your own emotions, and those of others, but you were not successful in doing so.

- What emotions did you have difficulty identifying in yourself and the other person or people?
- What skills would you like to have had so that you could have managed your emotions more effectively?
- What steps can you take now to develop skills?
- What would be the cost and benefits of taking these steps?[91]

Emotions are contagious

Being able to regulate your emotion is important to relationships because emotions can be contagious. We are happier in the company of happy people. This doesn't mean you can't be sad with your friends or share their difficulties, but regulating what you feel – when and where – affects how easy you are to be with. The more you notice your own behaviour and responses and understand what you are feeling, the better you get at understanding others. Actually, research shows that we are much better at assessing other people than ourselves; we tend to assess others more accurately because we actually see ourselves in a much better light. We appear to have illusions about how able and good we are; some research shows that there is a tendency to think we are more skilled and moral than, when tested, is actually the case.[92] This is especially true when it involves behaviour and responses that reflect what we value most. We are much better at judging others, especially when it comes to judging people's moral behaviour, than we are at assessing our own responses accurately. Judging others can mitigate and allow blindness to our self. In order to improve our empathetic skills one of the first things to question is our emotional judgement, of both ourselves and others.

Being judgemental

Why are we often so judgemental? Jonathan Haidt says it is because this is part of the essential glue that holds us socially cohesive. He argues that 'tit for tat', or 'Do as you would be done by', is the most successful way we have to work as an individual within a group; policing or monitoring this tension works through our common public judgement of each other. Because we assess and judge people, we hold them accountable and are in turn held accountable. We are constantly judging who is deserving of what reward or punishment, and we are naturally programmed to reciprocate like for like.[93] In his book, *Women are from Mars, Men are from Venus*, John Gray talks about how we are doing this in relationships all the time, subconsciously awarding points to ourselves and our partner.[94] Communication problems stem from the fact that we all have a different award system. There are many different award systems associated to gender, personality, class, culture, age, and most especially belief. What you believe, what you most value, reflect and govern how you make sense of the world and therefore affect your judgement and can govern your emotions.

We feel the world through what we value and we judge others through this veil of emotion.

⤴ brilliant exercise

Answer the following questions with a score of 1–10 to get an idea of how much you judge and compare yourself with others.

- How much do you feel let down by someone?
- How much do you criticise?
- How much do you praise?
- How much do you believe some people are worth spending time with?
- How much does it matter to you to be acknowledged?

Judging other people is one thing, judging yourself in reference to others is a first-class ticket to unhappiness.

Building a positive relationship with your romantic partner

There is a saying, 'The key to a happy marriage is to marry a happy person.' This is great advice – for the happy! Happy people are probably more likely to be married as they are more attractive and appealing. Happy people are also more likely to stay married as happiness and well-being indicate a more optimistic outlook, more resilience and therefore less likelihood of running for the door at the first sign of trouble. Being happily married is a good indicator of well-being and satisfaction with life and is also a contributing factor to health.[95]

 insight

Happiness comes first.

It is interesting to note that your individual happiness is only boosted by marriage for a couple of years, after which you return to your default happiness.[96] The hedonic treadmill kicks in! It appears from the research that the happier you are, the more likely you are to be and stay married as opposed to becoming happier if you get married.

In a well-known study, women in happy stable marriages in their middle age were found to be more likely to have photographs in their college year book that show them with a genuine warm (happy) smile. They were already happy.[97]

Being in a good relationship, however, is better than not being in a relationship, because in a relationship our basic need to feel connected, cared about and loved, which we examined in the last chapter, is met.

⊿ **brilliant** insight

We are happier with only one sexual partner and are likely to have more sex when in a stable monogamous long-term relationship.[98]

Is it all doom for the single and depressed? Of course not! The unhappiest people in relationship measures are those unhappily married. The last four chapters have hopefully already started to inspire you to a more positive way of living; the little things you can do to improve your confidence and well-being in other areas of your life can have a huge effect on your attractiveness to others, even if you have only decided to smile more and count your blessings more often. Being happily married is not the only ingredient of well-being.

brilliant tip

The most important ingredients in happy couples include:

- Respect.
- Acceptance.
- Believing that good qualities and positive behaviour are natural attributes of the other.
- Being specific rather than universal about conflicts. 'He was unkind today,' as opposed to 'He is always unkind.'
- Able to repair relationship issues and disputes quickly.
- Able to manage differing male and female conversational styles.
- Able to accommodate needs for intimacy and power.

Oscar Wilde called a cynic 'someone who knows the price of everything and the value of nothing'. Just praising your partner for their qualities is not enough; loving and valuing them include the gift of really seeing someone, their strengths as well as their weaknesses.

⟋ brilliant insight

Listening to ten minutes of a couple's conversation is enough for relationship expert John Gottman to say accurately who are destined for the divorce courts, just by listening to how they speak to and about each other. His research shows that for a flourishing relationship there need to be five positives to every negative. The hurt caused by negative emotions such as criticism, anger or hostility is five times more powerful than positive emotions such as interest, empathy or kindness. People who don't get cross or angry with their partners but also show no affection, no humour, and are uninterested in their partners are also not likely to last.[99]

Putting positive psychology to work with your partner and *all* close relationships

All the following subheadings are written in relation to a current partner; however, you will be able to see that many of the factors, questions and exercises apply equally to **all** close relationships, friendships and colleagues. As you work through the rest of the chapter, keep in mind a variety of people in your life that you would like a better relationship with.

1 Interest

Stop and think about how much interest you show your partner.

- What fun do you bring to your partner's life?
- What are they currently concerned about?
- How interested are you in their goals?
- Do you share adventures?

- Do you know how to surprise your partner?
- Find out something from your partner you didn't know; get curious but not intrusive.

Seeing the good, talking to and about people positively, sharing and showing interest, are all things that matter in any relationship, but most especially in romantic and long-term relationships.

2 Recognising your partner's and others' strengths

In the last chapter you looked at what were your top strengths. Now it is time to think about your partner's strengths and the strengths of those closest to you.

- Do you recognise and acknowledge your partner's qualities?
- Write your top five strengths and your partner's top five strengths.

- Which do you share?
- Which are different?
- How can you honour your partner's strengths?
- What is your partner's most important emotional need?

How could your answers become actions?

 Recognising someone else's strengths is not just good for them and for your relationship with them, it will make you happier too. This is not new, two thousand years ago the Roman emperor and philosopher

Marcus Aurelius suggested: *When you want to gladden your heart, think of the good qualities of those around you; the energy of one, for instance, the modesty of another, the generosity of a third and some other quality in another.* [100]

Marcus Aurelius, AD 121–180

3 Gratitude

Appreciating someone is part of really seeing them and what their being in your life gives you.

- Write down five things you love best about your partner.
- Now decide to tell them this week.
- What are you most grateful to them for?
- Tell them in a letter.
- What has this relationship taught you about yourself that you are grateful for learning?

4 Variety

Variety is the spice of life and applies to every chapter of this book.

- How can you surprise your partner this week that shows how much you know them, accept them and love them?
- What would be the most exciting thing your partner could do for you?
- What would it be like to tell them?

5 Look for the positive

Just as we adapt to our surroundings and situations (the problem of the hedonic treadmill from Chapter 2), so we can forget aspects of our partner that were once new and exciting.

- What first attracted you to your partner?

- Who were you then?
- What excited you?

6 Keep the bad things specific and the good things universal

Which two of the following four statements are you most likely to say?

1 My partner does things for me because he/she is kind, or
2 My partner was kind today because I needed help.
3 My partner was late because he/she missed their train, or
4 My partner always lets me down.

If you answered that you agree with 1 and 3 you are more positive than if you answered that you agree with 2 and 4. We will cover this subject in much more detail in the next chapter.

7 Healthy attachment

Some psychologists believe that how we love is laid down in childhood. The first relationship we develop is normally with our mother and the nature and health of this relationship can determine all our later relationships. The nature of our attachment to our mother can become the type of attachment we continue to make or can influence why we might be attracted to someone with a different attachment style.[101]

Attachment theorists assert that secure relationships are central to our intellectual, emotional, social and moral development: a child develops by exploring and adventuring beyond its mother; when the exploration becomes fearful the child returns to the mother before venturing forth again. A secure healthy attachment is formed when the child learns to trust the attachment and is able to become increasingly adventurous and autonomous. The attachment becomes unhealthy, *anxious* and needy, when the child doesn't receive comfort on return to the mother and continues to cling, uncomforted or not reassured. Some children avoid contact with the parent for whatever reason; this leads to an *avoidant* attachment style that is distant and uncomfortable with intimacy. Psychologists Cassidy and Shaver added a fourth type of attachment style which they describe as *disorganised,* which is a combination of both characteristics: detachment and clinging. Psychologist Alan Carr sees these same patterns of behaviour within families as well as in individuals.[102]

 **exercise**

Can you see which attachment style reflects your experience?

Secure	Anxious	Avoidant	Disorganised
Child is autonomous	Child is angry/clingy	Child is avoidant	Child is clingy and avoidant, fearful
Adult is autonomous	Adult is preoccupied	Adult is distant and dismissing	Adult is in conflict, ambivalent
Parenting is responsive	Parenting is intermittent, unreliable	Parenting is rejecting	Parenting is abusive or absent
Family is adaptable	Family is enmeshed	Family is disengaged	Family is disorientated[103]

Knowing your or your partner's attachment style can be the beginning of introducing important qualities to the relationship, such as understanding, acceptance, forgiveness and better emotional management. Attachment styles can also be a factor in the quality of friendship.

- What is your or your partner's attachment style?
- How might this be impacting your close relationships?

8 Celebration

Celebrating and sharing good things are a very important aspect of positive relationships. Sharing good things can be done well and encourage trust and intimacy. We all know how good it feels when someone says 'Well done', but it can feel even better when the 'Well done' is well done!

Being positive and supportive involves responding to good news in a genuine constructive reaction that actively acknowledges the other and celebrates the event with them. Psychologist Shelly Gable has shown that this is vital to the health and well-being of all relationships but particularly builds intimacy and trust.[104]

brilliant dos and don'ts

Do

✔ Be genuine and excited

✔ Mark the moment

✔ Be fully attentive and interested in all the details

✔ Really enjoy your friend's or partner's achievement

✔ Set your own needs aside.

Don't

✘ Talk about yourself and your achievements

✘ Look for bad consequences or pour cold water on it: 'That's great but how will you cope …?'

✘ Immediately change the subject or the focus of your attention

✘ Ignore the news or event.

Self-regard, your relationship with yourself

Accepting yourself, knowing and liking yourself, both allow your opportunities to grow and develop and also contribute to how you relate to other people. All theories of emotional intelligence highlight the importance of self-regard, and having a sense of your own identity.

Positive ways to build your self-regard

Avoid social comparison

We touched on this in Chapter 2 as maximisers tend to be more susceptible to the miseries of social comparison.[105] One of the most pertinent findings from many studies is that the happier you are, the less likely you are to notice or be affected by the success of other people.[106] Remember that constantly comparing yourself with other people is a quick route to misery. Research shows us that social comparison is one of the easiest ways to make ourselves feel depressed.[107]

Notice if you are constantly evaluating yourself in respect to other people. Your social support is part of who you are and those around you can have a great influence on how you feel about yourself. Being dependent on the opinions of others affects your own self-regard, which is then fed back into your relationships with other people.

⟋ brilliant exercise

Give a score of 1–10 for the following questions.

- How much does it matter to you that your friends think you live an interesting life?
- How much does it matter to you the amount of money you make in comparison to others?
- How much do you care about the car you drive?   ▷

▶ ● How much does it matter to you to have the right clothes, fancy or plain?

● How much does it matter to you to have the right furniture, scruffy or up to the minute?

● How much do you notice what books/films other people read or watch?

● How much do you notice other people's weight in relation to your own?

● How much do you notice other people's intellect?

● How much do you notice someone's spiritual awareness?

● How much do you want people to approve of you?

If you have scored highly answering these questions it could be that you care quite deeply about needing the approval of other people or that you validate yourself in comparison to others.

Comparing yourself and judging others is only bad when it is done negatively or makes us feel bad. We all need to feel we belong and we all love to belong to a 'tribe' we identify with, who share similar outlooks, pleasures and activities. Belonging to a football club, church community, sharing a school or geography, life experience or social class are part of who we are, and people who share these things with us share a part of our identity and make us feel we belong and are connected.

Wanting to have another identity from the one we 'think' we have is different from growing and developing an identity that is authentic and comfortable. Comparing yourself with others in a way that becomes unhealthy can develop from a belief that your identity comes from external expression, which can then become a life of constant neediness and judgement.

Make friends who share your values
Choosing relationships and friends that complement rather than compete with your own abilities and strengths stops you

being competitive and envious. Choosing partners and friends who have qualities and strengths you can admire and celebrate encourages reciprocal respect and admiration.

Be authentic rather than sincere

The idea of 'knowing who we are' in relation to what we think or value is relatively modern. We are increasingly identified by what we believe in. We are rewarded by outside approval of our sincere belief and adherence to socially acceptable ways of thinking. For Jonathan Haidt sincerity has become corrupted whereas authenticity, on the other hand, is rooted in reality; you can be high-minded and sincere, but to be authentic you must also be real, which requires compromise and full responsibility to both yourself and other people.[108]

People 'dripping with sincerity' feed on love and approval and we are drawn to the honest integrity of someone's sincerity. We even approve when someone is sincere about their belief in a damaging ideology, extreme self-expression or political decisions. The modern problem with sincerity is that it has lost its sincerity. As our identity becomes ever more dependent on others' approval, sincerity has become in the modern capitalist world what rhetoric became for the Greek philosophers: being *seen* as good or clever became more important than actually *being* good or clever. Sincerity now holds the same taintedness, thinking and believing who we want to be, rather than who we really are.

- Who are you when you are being sincere?
- Who are you when you are being authentic?
- How is this different?

Develop your self-regard through acceptance, love, curiosity, gratitude and fun. Learn to be and celebrate ALL that you are, your weaknesses, your strengths, your true origins and achievements. You will find yourself enjoying all your relationships better, especially with yourself. Learning self-acceptance is part of growing your self-regard.

Seeing and nurturing the best in other people

The most important quality you can bring to ALL your relationships is to see the best in other people. Victor Frankl uses the analogy of flying against a strong crosswind; you have to aim ahead of where you are going to get there because the wind is blowing you off course. Seeing other people this way has the same effect; seeing and believing in the full potential someone holds will support them becoming who they are, rather than seeing them 'as they are' and letting the headwind blow them back.[109]

⤴ brilliant insight

In a very powerful study, one teacher was given a class and told how lucky she was as she had all the bright children, and another teacher was told the opposite - bad luck, you have all the difficult stupid kids. Actually all the children had been randomly assigned to each class but the effect on the achievements of both classes was significantly different.[110]

Seeing the best in people and attributing good qualities and positive behaviour to someone's character is good not just for the person you are thinking about, but for your relationship with that person. This means not just attributing a quality to a specific act but seeing it as part of who they are: for instance, saying 'She was kind to me because she is kind,' rather than 'She was kind to me because I had had a bad day.'

 **recap**

- This chapter has introduced you to emotional intelligence and made you think about how you recognise, use, understand and manage your own and others' emotions.

- You have questioned how much you are judging both yourself and others.

- We looked at the ingredients of happy and healthy relationships and how gratitude, interest, celebration and variety are ways to positively improve your relationships.

- We have also looked at understanding your attachment style and how this can affect your relationships.

- We have looked at ways to build your own self-regard and started to examine why knowing who you really are matters to having a good relationship with yourself.

- We have also seen that how you attribute behaviour in yourself and in other people affects not only your relationships but your well-being and happiness. The next chapter will examine this more closely.

CHAPTER 6

How to become more resilient and cope better

Make the most of the best and the least of the worst.

Robert Louis Stevenson, 1850–94

If you have started to apply some of the findings from positive psychology in this book, you will already be building more self-resilience. This chapter will focus on the key qualities that build and foster resilience. We will look at why being optimistic helps you cope better than being pessimistic, what are the best coping defences, and how it is possible to grow from adversity and traumatic events.

brilliant tip

Positive psychologists have found that resilient people:

- Are optimistic
- Are hopeful and able to problem solve
- Believe in themselves but are not brimming with self-confidence
- Can self-regulate and use their emotions appropriately
- Are able to find benefit and meaning in adversity
- Use humour
- Have experience of a strong nurturing authority figure from childhood
- Use social support, are able to draw on friendships and family
- Have a good toolbox of adaptive defences
- Are able to learn, forgive and move on.

What is resilience?

Resilience implies more than just coping; resilience grows from *healthy* coping. All the chapters in this book will help you use the best of who you are to promote your well-being – remember, everything you do affects everything you do! As you learn to look on the bright side more, you will find yourself doing more, and, as you do more, you build small coping skills that become brilliant stepping-stones to cope with and bounce back from real adversity. And, with greater resilience, you will discover that you have more strength than you imagined, which will empower you to take on more and more challenges and to live a truly fulfilling life.

⟁ brilliant insight

Some top leaders who are resilient have spoken about not always feeling confident.[111] Resilient people are not necessarily more confident than other people, but have better coping strategies. Everyone thinks that being confident is the key to facing adversity, but, actually, we become better at coping at the same time as losing some of our confidence. Real life is a delicate adventure and the tough things both weaken and strengthen us. I think it is wonderfully liberating to know that resilience does not mean becoming a rock but actually is much more about learning how to bend appropriately.

Resilience is not the same as survival. Survival mechanisms may succeed in getting you through immediate or emotionally traumatic events, but, unless you work through the emotional after-effects, you won't necessarily learn from them or grow as a person. People who survive bankruptcy or job loss but see it only as failure rather than an opportunity for learning and growth are not resilient. Surviving a divorce is different from learning from what went wrong, letting go and building a new life on that knowledge. Resilience implies growth.

What makes a resilient person?

Many of our coping skills are laid down in childhood. Having a nurturing, protective but strong upbringing is a very strong factor in resilience. However, children can learn resilience vicariously and can be positively affected if there is at least one adult in their childhood who represents strong parenting and is supportive.[112] The skills we are born with are, of course, a factor. Children learn to problem solve and regulate behaviour from a very young age and can be taught to look on the bright side and develop a sense of humour. Children who are clever often learn to avoid being bullied through humour, getting on with other children is strong way of overcoming difficulties and trauma in childhood. Many comics say that their ability to make people laugh began as a coping strategy in childhood.

In Chapter 3 we looked at the importance of positive emotions in building our mental resources. Positive emotions therefore play a huge part in building and boosting our resilience. However, negative emotions (pain, grief, loss; all the emotions connected to suffering) are also the door through which we can develop and grow. As usual we need to know what it is we **really** feel and think in order to improve how we cope with both the small things that life throws up and the large.

The role of perception

The stories we tell ourselves and the explanations we give for events make up the narrative we live by. Positive psychologists have measured how much people's perception and interpretation of events affect how well they cope with adversity, both small and large.

The problem with accuracy

Pessimists and depressed people see things accurately, while optimists are more deluded about their abilities and their control over events.[113] The pessimist sees things 'as they are', but this appears from research to be a disadvantage, whereas the optimist's tinted sunglasses are a great defence in dealing with and responding positively to 'reality'. The pessimist can easily become overwhelmed and defeated but the optimist survives and thrives.

> We are actually more biased to seeing ourselves positively than negatively. We create a centre stage for ourselves and naturally we are the hero, the protagonist, the point of the unfolding story. Psychologist Shelley Taylor explains that when we hold positive illusions about ourselves, these illusions – rather than being a flaw in our perceptions – should be understood as a great resource and adaptive coping aid. Our healthy positive illusions protect us and allow us, in positive self-belief, to be more productive and effective, while a realistic analysis of our abilities may make us technically more 'sane' but less effective.[114]

Take the story of the mice who fall in the milk churn: the pessimistic mouse sees the hopelessness of his situation and quickly drowns, whereas the optimistic mouse keeps on swimming, believing that he is still in control of his environment and will triumph. He swims so hard and for so long that the milk turns to butter and he is able to jump out.

Having false illusions about your ability to change your environment does need a reality check and healthy optimists are quite able to face reality and in fact are more likely to do so. There are times when it is important to be both accurate about reality *and* our abilities, for instance when flying a plane, practising accountancy or operating on a patient; research shows that people are more accurate when slightly depressed or at least in a neutral mood, which appears to suggest that we need slightly pessimistic pilots, accountants and surgeons. However being optimistic, bigging it up a bit, can be a good thing and is especially so when we face adversity.

↗ brilliant insight

For Martin Seligman the importance of believing we can affect our own outcome whatever the circumstances came through his research into dogs' behaviour and their response to being mildly electrocuted. Many dogs gave up resistance quite quickly and resigned themselves passively to the treatment, while some continued to resist.[115] The ability to keep going despite continual setbacks and in the face of adversity is also a characteristic of human behaviour, as is the resigned helpless response. The difference between the two responses is the self-belief in the persistent group that they can still affect their situation. They remain optimistic and hopeful of their efforts to change their environment; it is the strength of this belief that carries them through adversity and challenge, while others give up.[116]

Attributional and explanatory style

The positive and negative thoughts you attach to outcomes and consequences affect the interpretations you give to what has already happened. These interpretations of the past can then become the projected emotions and expectations of what will happen. A negative interpretation of past or present events can become a pessimistic view of future events.

All the 'chatter' that makes up your 'story' can be either optimistic or pessimistic in tone; Martin Seligman calls this our 'attributional or explanatory style' and the good news is that you can change your attributional style – what you believe and the explanatory style that you talk about your belief.

Perceiving and interpreting situations and events matter to how we feel (Figure 6.1). How we *feel* influences our capacity to think clearly and affect our environment. How we *feel* determines our actions. If we interpret events negatively, or pessimistically, we function less well than those who have a positive or optimistic interpretation. Our *feelings* are dependent on what we **believe**. Therefore our ability to function well is dependent on what we choose to believe.

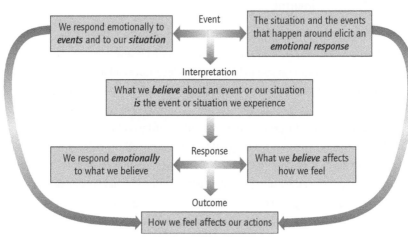

Figure 6.1 How interpretation and belief can change how we feel and respond

Taming the gremlin

There are many programmes that are based on noticing and changing beliefs. One of the most well established is cognitive behaviour therapy (CBT). There is an excellent book on CBT in the Brilliant series.

Seligman has also developed a programme based on earlier cognitive therapy models.[117] This is the Penn Optimism Program;[118] it has been used to great effect, especially helping children develop the ability to become better problem solvers, to become more hopeful and as a consequence less prone to depression. Seligman calls how we talk about what we believe our 'explanatory style'.[119]

What is your explanatory style? What is the 'chatter' in your ear telling you? As a coach noticing this chatter with my coaching clients I find it is helpful to give the voice a separate personality; a gremlin or a parrot, for instance. People even find it helpful to actually draw the gremlin. In different situations we draw on different experiences, and you may find that you have more than one 'gremlin'. The important thing is to practise listening to the voice in your head and noticing the story it is feeding you; then you can begin to 'turn the knob' appropriately or tame the gremlin.

The gremlin has three ways of talking to you negatively or pessimistically:

1 Permanence: always and never. (The sun never shines, he always lets me down.)

2 Pervasiveness: universal: all, everybody, everything. ((All) Diets are useless, all men are thoughtless.)

3 Personalisation: internally, me. (I'm no good, it's my fault.)

 **brilliant** example

What your pessimistic gremlin might believe vs an optimistic interpretation of a bad event

Bad event	Negative explanation (pessimistic)	Positive explanation (optimistic)
A friend cancelled lunch.	1 People always cancel.	1 She must be really busy today.
	2 Lunch dates are useless.	2 Lunch is difficult when you are working.
	3 She doesn't like me – it's because I am boring.	3 She often cancels.

How do we get to grips with our negative gremlins? Seligman follows Albert Ellis's model, what he calls ABCDE:[120]

- Adversity
- Beliefs
- Consequent mood change
- Disputation
- Energisation.

Using the above example, ABC become:

- Adversity = the friend cancelling
- Belief = she doesn't like me, deeper belief I'm boring
- Consequent mood change = now less happy than before.

The important idea is to start to notice which beliefs affect your mood. When the belief has been recognised it can then be examined for its veracity. What is the evidence for the belief? What is the consequent response to the belief?

D for disputation:

In this hypothetical example the disputation could be a number of things, such as:

- 'She often cancels'
- 'She never cancels'
- 'We see each other regularly'
- 'She said she was very busy when we made the arrangement'
- 'We have been friends for years'
- 'I don't know her well enough to judge yet', etc.

Each possibility has the potential to vary the interpretation of the event and consequently change the mood, with the desired outcome being to feel more positive about the event.

Beliefs should be questioned in two ways:

1 In relation to the adversity. Is the belief realistic? Is this the only interpretation of the evidence?

2 The consequent mood change. Is the emotional response out of proportion to the belief? When this is the case the belief may be an iceberg,[121] and underneath the surface is a more powerful hidden belief. This core belief may represent a core value, something that is a fundamental part of what matters most to you. See Chapters 4 and 7.

Understanding this basic principle, that our interpretation of events affects how we *feel*, is at the heart of knowing we can affect how we respond to and manage immediate events. When we see the world in a positive light we affect more than our immediate response.

> Each belief elicits a different emotional response. The gremlin can be very powerful. Karen Reivich and Andrew Shatte in their book, *The Resilience Factor*,[122] call these strong gremlins iceberg beliefs, because the surface response hides a bigger, deeper belief. You know you have hit an iceberg when your response is out of kilter with the event or situation. An iceberg is usually a belief that is linked to a deep need or strong value.

Building an optimistic explanatory style

Take a look at the following statements:

1 Permanence	Permanent	Temporary
	The weather here is always bad.	The weather here is bad today.
	I'll never get a job.	I didn't get that job because I was late.
	My life is great.	I had a really great day today.
	I am a great cook.	I cooked a great dinner tonight.

2 Pervasive	General	Particular
	I am no good.	I am no good at writing.
	She is beautiful.	She looks beautiful in that dress.
3 Personalisation	**Internal**	**External**
	I am boring.	You are no fun.
	I made that happen.	I was lucky.

These statements are examples of *both* positive and negative events that can be interpreted as *either*: particular or general; temporary or permanent; internal or external.

Look again at the positive and negative responses to the earlier bad event compared with positive and negative responses to a good event. Notice that in the bad event it is positive to make things temporary, specific and external but for a good event the opposite is true.

	Negative explanation (pessimistic)	Positive explanation (optimistic)
Bad event A friend cancelled lunch.	1 People *always* cancel. 2 Lunch dates are useless. 3 She doesn't like me – it's because I am boring.	1 She must be really busy *today*. 2 Lunch is difficult when you are working. 3 She is unreliable.
Good event A friend asks you to a party.	1 I got this invitation because it is her birthday. 2 This party sounds good. 3 What a surprise.	1 I often get asked to parties. 2 Parties are great. 3 I'm popular.

Be realistic about the bad events and over-egg the good ones.

- When you interpret something **bad** as *general, permanent or internal,* you are thinking with a pessimistic explanatory style.

- When you interpret something **good** with a *general, permanent or internal* explanation, you are thinking with an optimistic explanatory style.

In both cases the general permanent is *less* realistic than the particular and temporary interpretations. The important point to notice is that when a good thing happens, an optimist makes it permanent, general or personal while a pessimist leaves it as a temporary or particular event caused externally. When something bad happens, the optimist sees it as temporary or particular while the pessimist makes it permanent or general.

 brilliant example

It is when we face difficulties that optimistic thinking is most effective. My niece is a shining example of naturally seeing things as temporary and specific. When her breast implant failed after her mastectomy, rather than seeing it as compounding her problems, she was just relieved to be free of the pain. She saw it as it was, a single issue that could be put right at a later date, and in the meantime this mindset afforded her respite from the uncomfortable weight it had become. She also found a benefit, which we will come to.

Start to notice your explanatory style:

- When you use enduring or permanent interpretations of situations

- When you use universal or general interpretations of events

- When you are too specific, particular or exact about something good that you have achieved

- When you give credit to fate or luck rather than your ability or effort.

This is not an invitation to become delusional! As with all things, the trick is to mitigate the thinking that spirals us downwards and to reinforce the thinking that spirals us upwards. We just need to turn the knob appropriately.

 insight

The research is still varied on the extent to which being more negative and emotionally distressed *before* an event affects the responses *to* an event but there is enough research to underpin the basic fact that positive or negative thinking influences either an upward or downward spiral.

The power of optimism

Most positive psychologists agree that it is our expectations of the future that affect the outcome. Having a positive perception and interpretation of situations and events and the part we play matters. Optimists really do fare in adversity much better than pessimists! Situations get better with a more optimistic outlook and reducing pessimistic thinking improves well-being and your ability to cope better.[123]

Research into many different aspects of psychological well-being has shown that being optimistic can:

- Reduce anger
- Reduce loneliness and give a greater feeling of control in old age

- Reduce daily hassles and lower stress
- Reduce depression: after childbirth, in cancer and for Alzheimer's caregivers
- Allow better adjustment to new environments
- Reduce the likelihood of depression after amputations
- Afford higher self-esteem
- And even limit fear and anxiety after experiencing a missile attack![124]

As the above list suggests, optimists appear to cope better, and through being optimistic they are actively mentally encouraging healthier recovery from illness and adversity.

Optimism also positively affects our ability to:

- Build resilience for the future
- Grow from small and large events
- Create opportunities
- Have better relationships
- Reorder priorities and make better goals.

brilliant insight

Psychologists Carver and Schreier see optimistic thinking as a disposition. They have found through years of research that being disposed to look on the bright side is definitely an asset and that the more pessimistic your outlook, the more likely you are to suffer not only from more illness generally but also depression and loneliness.[125]

Optimism is not the opposite of pessimism:

● We can lessen our negative thinking while not increasing our positive thinking.[126]

● And vice versa, we can increase our optimistic thinking without lessening our pessimistic thinking[127]

● The trick is to do both: reduce pessimistic thinking and increase optimism.

 **brilliant** tip

You can test how optimistic you are at www.authentichappiness.com and take the free optimism test.

Coping optimistically and building your resilience

1 Problem solving

Overcoming any adversity or situation requires that we can assess the situation and find different routes through it. Being better able to cope involves both the ability to problem solve and the emotional capacity to stress-manage the situation. As we saw in Chapter 4 on achieving goals, being able to problem solve is an important coping strategy, so keeping in mind all the factors that support your ability to problem solve is also building your coping skills. Having an optimistic interpretation of your situation allows you to problem solve better. Optimists, like the mouse, have the ability to imagine positive outcomes, or believe they can influence their situation. They continue to see possibilities and act on them rather than acting 'in defence' or simply accepting negative interpretations. People who continue to act this way experience less stressful and less negative emotions. We have seen in Chapters 3 and 4 the cognitive effect of positive feeling. Thinking is part of the means of being able to imagine more and better solutions; finding ways to boost positive feeling helps you think better and as you think better you are more imaginative. The hopeful feedback loop is activated.

 insight

Positive pessimism

Just to be confusing, it is not all about optimism. When we are coping with adversity and stress, 'unrealistic' optimism is not healthy optimism. While remembering that looking for the worst in situations has been shown to be a bad strategy, some people manage difficult and stressful challenges with defensive pessimism. This actually fuels better thinking as it is a way of coping that identifies worst-case scenarios in order to anticipate things and have a strategy ready. People who think this way actually cope less well if they are instructed to think positively.[128] Defensive pessimism is a form of problem solving that involves careful assessment and thought about how to handle anxiety; as long as the problems are examined as challenges to overcome, rather than to succumb to, it is an effective coping mechanism.

2 The support of others

Optimists are much more likely to seek the support and advice of others; this is both emotionally strengthening and also reduces the risk of putting into effect reactions and strategies that might be over-optimistic or unrealistic. Turning to friends and family can also give support and encouragement to good plans and emotional self-management. Pessimists are more likely to withdraw from other people.

3 Engage with the problem

Optimists are not positively in denial; in fact, they tend to be more realistic than pessimists and this is key to the other big factor in optimistic behaviour: ***engagement***. Optimists engage rather than distance themselves from life's problems, seeing things as challenges to be overcome rather than problems to be avoided. *Healthy* optimists, remember, are realistic as well as optimistic in dealing with adverse situations; they see things as they are. Having faced the issue, it is easier to think rationally and positively about a response because reality is kept in check. In order to do this, we need to practise constructive thinking: learning how to think in a way that promotes positive thought beyond the rational assessment of a situation.

4 Benefit finding

Optimists are more likely to find benefits; finding benefit when things go wrong is a great coping tool. There are two ways of looking for benefits: the first is to imagine the worst-case scenario and compare this to the actual event in order to see things in a better light. Secondly, actively look for some positive aspect of an event or situation on which to focus. These are both good coping strategies. Finding benefit as a consequence of an adverse event supports both the way the event is viewed in the long term and the ability to cope better in the future. Benefit finding is key to growing out of adversity, whether it is short-term relief or a positive slant to the longer-term process. Finding benefit from understanding what happened has a place and purpose in the bigger picture of your whole story.

brilliant exercise

Think of a problem or difficulty that you are currently dealing with:

- Can you find benefit in this adversity that you are presently dealing with?

- What one good consequence has this situation given you?

- How can you see things in a more positive way?

Optimists accept reality better, and perhaps because they are more delusional about their ability to affect their environment they are more positively emotionally engaged so that they are better able to problem solve. They see things in a positive way, look to others for support, find meaning in the situation and are prepared to learn. Pessimists, on the other hand, tend to hide from reality, despite assessing the situation accurately, and are more likely to disengage emotionally and use avoidance strategies.

Emotional coping strategies

When things get tough our emotions go into overdrive, and people who are able to handle their emotions in adversity are more likely to fare better.

Adaptive defence mechanisms

Adaptive defence mechanisms are behaviours we employ to control our emotions in stressful situations. The psychologist George Vaillant suggests that we use the following five:[129]

- **Suppression**. Are you able to put your feelings aside until you are able to let them loose in an appropriate way? Suppressing emotion long term is not good for you, but equally being able to stay calm – 'keep your head when all around are losing theirs' – is an important coping skill. Practise small techniques like breathing and composing yourself before speaking and notice your posture – if you are standing in either an aggressive or defeated manner you will find that the emotion is harder to suppress. Practise arranging your body and muscles into the emotion you need to support yourself.

- **Anticipation.** How good are you at anticipating situations and being prepared? Real problem solving thinks ahead as much as in the heat of the moment. Being able to anticipate situations in order to mitigate the outcome is common sense: prepare for the worst but more importantly anticipate the best and prepare for that too. Having an open mind and a growth mindset will help you anticipate, look for and be ready for opportunities in the midst of adversity.

● **Altruism.** This is a brilliant coping strategy at every level. If you are looking out for someone else it is much harder to worry about yourself. Can you leave your own worries and troubles aside and give yourself up to dealing with supporting someone else? Why not make a habit of giving your time in some way? (Looking after other people's needs as an emotional coping strategy is very powerful but be careful not to let it develop into *needing* to be needed too much.)

● **Humour.** Humour is a key strategy to reduce stress and also supports other coping strategies such as easing the process of facing up to things. Research indicates that humour contributes to relieving stress and supporting recovery from illness. Humour is a good coping strategy because laughter affects us physically and while you are laughing you are doing yourself a power of good. Also, remember that it may make you think better as well as relieve your stress.

⤢ brilliant insight

Humour is a difficult subject and multifaceted. Humour can be hostile as well as positive.[130] Many comedians suffer from depression. Men and women also use humour differently; men are more likely to use humour to divide, whereas women use it more to bring people together.[131]

- **Sublimation.** Are you able to divert your emotions into more socially acceptable guises? Conflict and passion alike can be channelled into an artistic outlet or diverting activity. When your emotions are high, are you able to allow them voice in a valid but subliminal activity?

 **exercise**

Think of the last stressful situation you can remember being in.

- Did you employ any of the above adaptive defence mechanisms?
- Would humour have helped?
- Did you focus on yourself or see anyone else's problems?
- Is there anything you could have anticipated better?
- How could you have handled the situation better?

Accommodating and reframing

Reframing is another way of talking about changing how we see events. Coming to terms with adversity in a healthy way relies not only on finding meaning in the event but in accommodating what has happened in a way that allows it to build something into our lives rather than to be pushed under the carpet. When we absorb a changed status or adversity, we can absorb or assimilate it as if nothing has changed; the event or situation must be required to fit with how we are. Small events and setbacks are easy to absorb, but things can happen to us after which it is not so easy to carry on as if nothing has happened. Death, serious illness, loss of wealth, even loss of country – any trauma after which our identity and our sense of who we are and what we are doing are significantly changed – require that we are able to accommodate this changed state of affairs. Having a growth mindset rather than a fixed mindset is one of the most important factors in being able to accommodate and grow out of life-changing events.

Being able to accommodate adversity is like taking a shirt that no longer fits and using the material as part of a beautiful patchwork. The shirt is still there; it is no longer useful as a shirt but it is too precious to be discarded, so rather than try to force it to continue to serve its original purpose it is allowed to change and in doing so retains its value. We too can learn to do this when life deals us blows and challenges that change us and our circumstances such that is better to accommodate the change and reshape ourselves rather than to carry on as if nothing has happened. For example, to assimilate the loss of your legs would be to continue to act and be exactly the same with the inconvenience of being in a wheelchair. On the other hand, accommodating the change allows you to develop new ways of living that take account of your changed status in a way that builds all the best of who you were before into the new person you have become.

Post-traumatic growth

After adversity or a traumatic event, it is possible to become *more* than you were before; growing out of suffering is something that is not just the staple of Hollywood scriptwriters. Changing for the better out of pain is at the heart of religious and philosophical teaching, and of great literature. This potential is one of the most powerful experiences of the human condition. Measured and examined under the title post-traumatic growth, psychological change following trauma and adversity has been a recognised effect for many years. When this term was first used by psychologists Tedeschi and Caloun in 1996 they were using the concept to combine past psychological reports of growth from adversity with results from their own clinical experience.

Psychological change can be described as post-traumatic growth when people describe experiencing some of the following aspects:

- Improved relationships

- New possibilities for their lives
- A greater appreciation of life
- And a greater sense of personal strength and spiritual development.[132]

 **insight**

Personal losses can produce:

- a growth in character
- a growth in perspective
- better relationships.[133]

Good from bad – this process carries paradoxes:

- People experience both their weakness and their vulnerability at the same time as finding strength and capability.
- People experience directly the best and the worst in others; they find out what people they know are really made of.
- Through the need to speak of what has happened, people learn the role of intimacy and who they can talk to, and in sharing become more compassionate.
- People learn what really matters and become more appreciative of the small things.
- People report that they examine life's meaning and find a more spiritual context to live by.[134]

That things such as the above are possible is inspiring, but post-traumatic growth is dependent on many things and is not immediate. These things happen over time and the suffering and pain of some events can be so considerable that to go into real detail in this way is much more than this book is capable of. One interesting aspect of research is the effect that writing things down can have, as opposed to just dealing with the facts and emotional responses.[135] It is interesting to note that Marcus Aurelius, the Roman emperor, talks of getting his generals to write of and share with each other their experiences immediately after battle.

Talking about trauma helps to make sense of what has happened and offers the opportunity to find benefit. Research conducted by psychologist James Pennebaker has shown the effect of writing about trauma creates the opportunity to make sense and find meaning. He asked people to write for 15 minutes a day over a week about an event that had been difficult or traumatic. After a year those who had worked through the exercise were healthier than the control group who just kept a diary and also healthier than those who had just written without finding meaning or perspective. Just writing isn't enough; it is making sense that matters.

 **brilliant** exercise

Try James Pennebaker's writing exercise:

'For the next four days I would like you to write about your very deepest thoughts and feelings about the most traumatic experience of your life. In your writing, I'd like you to really let go and explore your very deepest emotions and thoughts. You might tie your topic to your relationships with others, including parents, lovers, friends or relatives. You may also want to link your experience to your past, your present or your future, or to who you have been, who you would like to be, or who you are now. You may write about the same general issues or experiences on all days of writing or on different traumas each day. All will be completely confidential.'[136]

Don't worry about what you write, about spelling or grammar, just let your feeling flow onto the page. This is for your eyes only. Try not to rant.

The need for all experience to be expressed

Recovery and growth are most likely to happen within an environment that allows expression of *all* the processes of thought and emotions; a social or cultural environment that does not constrain being able to acknowledge all feelings, thoughts and experiences. Being properly heard supports the narrative process that can then become a new life story. It is also important that being heard and understood happens without any pressure to solve what can't be solved but allows the process of accommodation and change to develop. Being with other people who have had similar experiences and grown in some way can inspire growth in others.

Sense of coherence

Getting a better sense of coherence comes from knowing what really matters to us in a way that offers a clearer focus on our life; a context into which everything else fits. All the unimportant clutter gets swept away as a life comes into service to a why. Sometimes we are living in a way that feels like disjointed pockets. The psychologist Aaron Antanovsky believes having a sense of coherence in our lives is a contributing factor to being satisfied with life. With a sense of coherence our life has more cohesion, makes sense in a meaningful way and is therefore more manageable. People can develop a greater sense of coherence in their lives out of adversity because frivolous and meaningless activities can fall away.

---

brilliant example

A friend has turned years of coping with a severely disabled daughter into a charitable project. Her personal experience of tragedy and suffering is now her greatest strength in meeting the needs of others through her work, which is also exciting and challenging. She is living an adventure she ▶

▶ couldn't have imagined some years ago. All the unimportant aspects of her life have fallen away and she has a much clearer focus that unites all that she does to a common purpose. She has a 'why', and the why has come from a painful experience.

 He who has a why to live can bear with almost any how.

Friedrich Nietzsche, 1844–1900

In this chapter I have mainly been talking about adversity and trouble in the singular. However, many people today are dealing with more than one difficulty. The effect of an accumulation of adversity such as poverty, abuse or absence of a parent shows that the more 'risks', the lower the IQ becomes in adolescents.

Research by the psychologist Arnold Sameroff found with no adversities the average IQ score is 119, with only one risk factor the IQ scores were 116, with two risk factors 113, with four the IQ scores plummet to 93 and with 8 it is as low as 85. Most children can thrive with one or two adversities or 'risk factors' but the greater the number the bigger the effect in their IQ scores.[137]

Losing cognitive skills is to lose the most vital factor for building hope and resilience. As we have seen, we also need to be able to problem solve and to think around and with our emotions. Remember, at the beginning of this chapter we reminded ourselves of the importance of positive effect and that experiencing positive emotion is a key factor in how we build our resources. Remember also from Chapter 3 that there is a tipping point for positivity that can literally turn the dial the other way. Research confirms the accumulative effect for 'assets', and assets include everything in this book.

On the resilience of adolescents Arnold Sameroff tells us:

Of the kids who had 31 to 40 assets, only 6% were found to be in the violent category. Of the kids who had 21 to 30 assets, 16% were in the violent category. Of the kids who had 11 to 20 assets, 35% were in the violent category. And of the kids with zero to 10 of these assets, 61% were in the violent category. The issue is not which asset you have, but, rather, the number of assets you have.[138]

 **brilliant** recap

In this chapter you were introduced to how your beliefs affect how you react and respond to events and why having an optimistic outlook helps you cope better and become more resilient.

- It encouraged you to examine your beliefs and to think about ways to build a more optimistic approach to living.
- You have looked at your explanatory style and been reminded that keeping the bad things specific, temporary and external can help you cope better when things go wrong.
- You have been introduced to the ABCD model to help you examine and understand your explanatory style and help you build a more optimistic interpretation.
- We have looked at four optimistic coping mechanisms:
  1   Problem solving, a review of Chapter 4
  2   Use the support of other people, share your problems
  3   Engage with the problem, face up to things
  4   Find benefit in your adversity.
- We have also looked at five emotional ways to cope by using:
  1   Suppression
  2   Anticipation

▶

3 Altruism

4 Humour

5 Sublimation.

● We have examined why it is good to be able to accommodate adversity and that writing and finding meaning aid recovery from trauma.

● This chapter has taken you from small coping strategies to dealing with life trauma. It is important to develop strategies that work for you and strengthen them. Everything in this book is about building positive assets that support your abilities to become more resilient and to thrive whatever your circumstances.

Developing a 'can do', optimistic outlook is a very good place to start. The next chapter builds on finding the 'why', the purpose in your life.

CHAPTER 7

Find out what matters: Having purpose in your life

The purpose of life is a life of purpose.

Robert Byrne

This chapter will help you discover better what you truly value, what gives your life its meaning and purpose.

Why do we need meaning/purpose?

It does not take positive psychologists to tell us that a flourishing happy life is made up of more than just transitory good feelings, and doing what we like best. We cannot live only as ungoverned pleasure seekers. Much of what brings us the most joy can be things we struggle to achieve and choose to address for long-term rewards.

Remember that all experiences contain an irony in that we adapt very quickly: 'the hedonic treadmill'. This speedy adaptation to our experiences has both good and bad consequences. Something you once desired, which you now have and that initially gave you great pleasure, you quickly become used to. The pleasure doesn't last; we adapt and require something else. That new dress, car, kitchen, even job or partner, which was once the answer to everything, can become mundane and ordinary; equally, you can adapt to bad things – you are able to tolerate and even stop noticing things that initially gave you pain.

Joy and happiness that last come from living in a meaningful and purposeful way, such that the joy and satisfaction you experience are not dependent on satiating your transient desires. Knowing that what you do in life matters, or at least has some purpose if only in a small way, will give fulfilment and richness in your life. Much of what gives your life its meaning is right in front of you. Many of the positive interventions that affect well-being are in some way encouraging you to look again at your life through newer, or older, eyes, to remind yourself of the good things you have and to challenge your complacencies.

Research has repeatedly linked positive health benefits to finding meaning in your life. The benefits of making meaning include:[139]

- Able to change perceptions from unfortunate to fortunate
- Improved mental health
- Improved self-worth
- Gives life a purpose, a coherent story
- Improves immunology.

Having meaning in your life gives you the 'why' you do what you do. Knowing that your life has meaning helps you face up to difficulties and overcome hardship. The meaning, 'your story', defines your role, making who you are, and what you do, matter.

 Lack of meaning and purpose accounts for much of the rise in depression in America.

Victor Frankl, 1905–97

Victor Frankl, a holocaust survivor, remarks in his seminal book *Man's Search for Meaning* that lack of meaning and boredom in people's lives causes more mental health problems than distress.[140]

Knowing what you value, and living to those values, gives meaning and purpose to what you do. Living a purposeful life has direction; you know the path you are on and equally importantly *who* you are. **You** are the path you walk: when your path is more important than the destination, life becomes vibrant and exciting; you know where you are headed and why. Your path is not so much about goals and work but the quality you bring to the process of living – your purpose, your unique contribution.

What is your path? Is it a path with a heart? There is no point in rushing along always looking to the goals ahead only to find when you get there that it was the wrong path. How do you find your path, your purpose? It is not always easy to know exactly what this is. This chapter will help you develop an understanding of *what* you truly value and *why* you value it, so that you can develop more meaning and purpose to your own life.

brilliant insight

People who have a purpose to their life live longer and are more likely to be mentally well for longer. With a long-term study, psychologist Aron Buchman looked at what positive aspects of life are associated with a decreased risk of Altzeimer's. Those who scored highly on having a purpose to their lives were 2.4 times less likely to develop Alzeimer's than those who had average scores, and it was the only factor that significantly showed any effect.[141]

How to find meaning

You have looked at using your strengths, doing things that give you the opportunity to be in flow and feel intrinsically motivated. You have challenged your mindset, looked for meaning in things you have overcome and thought about how you can enjoy more of life's everyday pleasures. You are perhaps a little more positive, hopeful and grateful. But how do you find that magic thing, the role in life that you want to do because it holds a deeper meaning and a purpose beyond yourself? What you value and what holds the most importance for you are the first way we will explore your life purpose. Values are the way we all prioritise needs. Needs are universal but how we prioritise those needs is individual and unique. We can all value love, family, honesty, trust, kindness, fun or security; however, the closer we get to values that really resonate, the easier it is to live authentically. The list of values at the end of the book numbers over 300 and it is worth spending time on the exercises to come to really flush out not just your strengths but your unique purpose.

brilliant tip

- Living with someone else's values is not as good as living with your own.
- Feeling good is not the same as feeling fulfilled.
- Doing 'good things' and living a 'good life' are not good if they are something you are imposing on yourself.

brilliant insight

Research has shown that living congruently with our values positively affects our well-being, especially when the values expressed are authentic to the individual and come from within. More intrinsic, autonomous and achievement-orientated values (e.g. novelty, change, excitement, self-expression or passion) are more likely to positively affect well-being. Some of the more extrinsic values (e.g. tradition, order or stability) can have a negative effect. Nonetheless, it is not the case that happiness and well-being come only from within; what we are learning scientifically is that we experience happiness and well-being from external-related needs as well as from internal self-expression.[142]

Knowing your purpose, what gives your life its unique meaning, however, is an intrinsic, internal process.

Take a quick overview of your life and see where you experience most meaning and fulfilment:

- With family and friends
- In your career or at work
- When engaged with your hobbies and recreation
- Keeping your life on track, balancing your accounts, paying your bills
- Keeping healthy, exercising, eating well, visiting the dentist
- With your partner
- In your home environment, or outside with nature
- Within a wider community, voluntary work, political activities
- Within your spiritual life.

Note from 1 to 10 how much your life purpose shows up in each different area of your life.

Increasingly research is revealing that we have multiple sources of meaning, our values and needs change as we change, and what we value in one area of our life is different from another. We can be multifaceted **and** authentic;[143] we can integrate ourselves to our lives in a coherent way. Having a sense of purpose is the most powerful way we can do this.

Take a moment to revisit the list you made in Chapter 4, listing your top strengths. Your top strengths are an expression of your values. From this list, think about what you really value; what qualities, attributes can you not live without? What really matters to you so much that you must have this in your life? Revise and expand your original list to make it your top 20 values and put them in order of importance. Have a look at the list of values in the appendix to get an idea of what to put down. When you have a list, score each from 1 to 10 based on how much this value shows up in your life.

Go back over your list and ask yourself:

- How many things on the list did you write because you were brought up to value these things?
- How many things on the list did you write because you felt you ought?
- What did you leave off because you were uncomfortable giving it voice?

The next few exercises and questions are also ways to unpack what matters to you and to discover what you value within the context of your life.

⟋ brilliant insight

When we are young we often inherit our parents' values and many people continue for years living a life someone else has given them. Our experiences also shape our needs; for example, if you grew up in an environment where you were afraid, you might well need safety above everything. Finding your life purpose requires that you are able to differentiate emotional needs that are a consequence of past experience from needs that fulfil your potential and give meaning to what you do. Some of the values that we have been brought up with and are a part of who we are may not fit us any more because our needs are different from those of our parents. Because values help us prioritise our needs and often give us the reason 'why' we do things, they can have cultural and linguistic meaning and importance.

Values that identify us socially and culturally

Values are also increasingly socially imposed and are part of socially accepted norms. As people become more and more identified by what they value, the values themselves hold cultural currency. It is to this last point that the psychologist Oliver James addressed his book, *Affluenza*,[144] which examines why people are so unhappy despite having so much. If what we value is merely a reflection of what we think we ought to value, we will not flourish.

We inherit much of our value structure

Words have meaning but what *actually holds meaning* for **us** is the *'why'* in our lives. The 'meaning', why we 'care' about something and what we 'feel' can be culturally, socially and individually influenced. For example:

- Religious and conservative values are inclined to incorporate tradition, group conformity, respect for authority, purity of the body, humility and the needs of others.

- There are different value structures within different religions. For example, Protestant values hold a strong work ethic and sense of justice (the German sociologist Max Weber argued that it was Protestant religious ideals that underpinned the growth of capitalism, bureaucracy and a rational-legal state[145]).

- Business values encourage performance, power and achievement, creativity, productivity and excellence.

- Western liberal values are more about freedom of expression, individualism and fairness for all.

- Some national cultures can value generosity and hospitality above everything, while for other cultures self-discipline and respect are paramount.

- Nihilists hold no values!

▶

▶

● Families hold some values over others – honesty,
   accomplishment, independence or trust. A strong parent can
   instil the need for order and safety to such an extent that
   children either rebel and long for chaos and adventure or
   conform and adopt the same values.

**No value is wrong, but it is important to understand where some
of your values may originate.**

↗ **brilliant** exercise

Answer the following questions to find the values that have been given to
you.

● Write down the values and needs you grew up with. _____

● What were your parents' most important values? _____

● What ethos and principles did your school give you? _____

● What have you learnt to value in your line of work? _____

● What do you most value in work, college and associates? _____

● What values are an important ingredient in your religion if you
   have one? _____

● What values are central to your political opinion? _____

Look hard at what you have written. Which of these answers are important
to you?

Do you want to let go of anything that no longer serves you or may be
stopping you living more fully?

How do the answers to these questions match your top ten?

These questions are about values that you have had around you. If
answering any of these questions was either hard or revealing, use the
answer to review your list.

Finding what we need and value is just the beginning!

Finding who we are beneath and beyond all the cultural and social masks is where we find our unique life purpose. Some people say it is a very quiet voice; your life purpose is your soul's work and your soul can be shy; however, sometimes this voice is very loud.

Now answer the following questions:

- If you had one wish for yourself, what would it be? _____
- What do you wish for others? _____
- If you bestowed a wish on a stranger on the street, what would it be? _____
- What games did you play as a child? What did you love doing as a child? _____
- What do others say is your passion? _____
- What is your passion? _____
- What do people turn to you for? _____
- What do you stand for? _____
- What is the worst way someone could treat you? _____
- How do you honour someone? _____
- What need are you most called to respond to? _____
- What suffering in the world most calls to you? _____
- Have you ever risen to an occasion or stepped up unexpectedly? _____
- Can you remember a time, a moment, when everyone looked to you and what you were doing seemed as natural as breathing? Write down what you were doing, where you were, who you were with and the most important features of the context and environment. All contributing factors that made you fly. _____

- Can you remember a significant flow or peak experience? Write down where and when this was and what you were doing. _____

_____

 **exercise**

Try this visualisation.

Find a quiet moment. Relax, close your eyes and imagine that you are 102 and this is a party to celebrate your life. Many people are there and you have the chance to get up and speak. When you get up to speak what you say has an enormous impact. People are even changed in some way.

Then write down the answers to the following questions

- What is it about you that everyone loves?

  _____

- What are they celebrating about you?

  _____

- What was the impact you made?

  _____

You now have a lot of information about the things that matter to you, what is important – and even some descriptive prose.

- Is there a recurring thread to your answers?
- Has anything surprised you?
- What answers, if any, prompted an emotional response?

 **exercise**

Steve Pavlina[146] has an interesting way to discover your life purpose. The exercise will take anything from 30 to 60 minutes and is worth the time.

I know people who have been more than sceptical and have found it amazing. Make sure you are undisturbed.

Take a blank sheet of paper or computer screen, write 'What is my life's true purpose?' at the top and start writing; write anything that comes into your head, and just keep writing until you cry. As you write, notice when you feel a surge of emotion and mark it so that you can return to it. Numbering each statement is helpful and be prepared to go to 100 and beyond if necessary. If you dry up or get stuck, stop, take a two-minute break and return. Good luck.

Create a mission statement

We don't find it strange that a good business knows what they do, who they do it for and have a mission statement that can sum up the ethos of what they are about, something unique that is represented at every level of production or service. Brand awareness is predicated on this principle and when the brand delivers on its promise both customer and staff can trust and enjoy their connection and involvement with the product.

- Do you have a mission statement and, if you do, does it fit into your life?

Finding your true purpose can be a little like a good mission statement, but any old statement about 'love', 'family' and 'kindness' won't do. A mission statement has to resonate uniquely for **you**; it must sum you up so that when you hear it you feel energised and alive. Look carefully at all your responses to the questions and exercises: can you see a mission statement, a reason that you can meet this need in the world? Use at least five values and put them in a context that is your unique 'why'. Don't feel you have to come up with the perfect mission statement straight away. Remember that the growth mindset is open to learning and is curious. Use your strengths and notice when you feel emotion, and when it is easy and fun.

Keep it simple if you find this too overwhelming. Notice any exercises in this book that made you feel more alive.

Living authentically

Being in an environment where you can live congruently with those things that mean most to you affects your overall satisfaction with life. If you work or live in an environment that is completely at odds with everything you care about and value, do not be surprised if you are unhappy! Living congruently to your values is the beginning of stepping into an authentic life.

↗ brilliant insight

Research tells us that our happiness and satisfaction with life are better when personal values are matched to environments that emphasise those same values.

People in seminary school who held 'benevolence', 'conforming' and 'care' values were happier than those who emphasised the need for 'power' and 'self-expression'. The opposite was true for trainee managers.[147]

If you are living at odds with everything that matters to you, what can you do about it? Can you bring more of your own purpose and meaning into your everyday life? For example, if you have noticed that you value being connected to nature and you love being part of a committed team (perhaps loyalty and kindness are your strengths), then your true life purpose might be to educate the world about the beauty of nature, to protect those who cannot protect themselves and to see the joy in people. You will struggle with a job in the city. However, your life purpose can still be met if you are able to use your free time to engage in outdoor activities and you are able to bring fun and laughter and a sense of care to your day-to-day exchanges.

How to get meaning and direction into your life:

- Use your strengths.
- Find a 'why' – why what you are doing has a part in your story.
- Write your life as a story in the third person.
- Find one thing you believe in.
- Notice patterns in your life.
- Use guilt, sadness and pain as opportunities for growth and change.

Telos

Philosophers speak of having a *telos*. Having a telos is the purposeful direction of not just our skills and abilities but also their complete integration with our growth in character in the same purposeful direction. Having a telos relied as much on your good character and social reputation growing and developing as on your expertise and professional abilities. Having a telos describes a whole life in development, both social and professional. A telos is the integration of character and skill; the expertise and personal qualities of someone **ARE** who they are. Today we speak more about having a calling, a vocation. The word vocation literally means a calling.

- What are you called to do?

Money and fame

What if the thing that matters above everything is money and fame? If money is what matters most, think about *why*. What will that money buy you? What are you seeking? Is it security, excitement, recognition, peace or material goods? If it is 'things', what will these things mean to you and why do you want them? What would you get if you got these things? Who would you be if you had these things? The answers to these questions contain what really matters to you.

Valuing money is important, but money is much more than something to be desired in itself. It doesn't matter how much we earn, we tend to spend what money comes our way on what we most value.

How we spend the money we have reflects:

- Our time persectives
- The way we think
- What we value
- What we really care about.

The more we understand what is of real value to us, the less likely we are to invest in short-term happiness hits.

If you desire and need money, what would having more money give you? Now answer what would having **that answer** give you? And again what would **that answer** give you? Keep answering until you find what you really need more of.

Look again at your list earlier and see if you spend your money on what you most value. How could you spend your money in a way that reflects what is really meaningful to you?

brilliant insight

What you spend your money on is very often what you value. It doesn't matter how much you earn - if you don't value money itself, it will fly out as fast as it flies in, on the things you DO value!

The more you know what really matters to you and you have meaning and purpose to your life, the more you will care about what you invest in financially.

Your purpose in life could be to *become* rich and many people become rich living an authentic life using their talents and strengths. However, if there is no meaning beyond the extrinsic reward of money, the level of well-being and satisfaction with life is not as great as for those who are doing what they love *and* making money.

brilliant insight

As we noted at the beginning of this book, research shows that if we can pay our bills and earn an average wage, the amount of income increase after this has very little effect on happiness. People with more money are only slightly happier and in fact when people get very rich their happiness levels can actually reduce.

The cost of materialistic values

Several studies have found that the more materialistic people are, the less happy and satisfied with life they are. They are also more likely to be distressed, depressed, anxious, narcissistic, and more unhealthy than people who are less materialistic.[148]

Psychologist Tim Kasser highlights the cost of material values not only to ourselves but to relationships. Materialistic people are less empathetic and less generous and more likely to see people as commodities to help them get on in life or to give them the right social image. Being materialistic makes people much more status conscious and we have seen that comparison with others is detrimental to our well-being and happiness.[149]

Remember the research quoted in the first chapter, that people were happier after giving money away than spending it!

> The more money people have and the more focused they are on money the less able they are to savour things.

 **brilliant** tip

Decide to turn the television off and stop buying magazines, as soaking up constant advertising messages feeds materialism.[150]

Positive psychology is showing very clearly that happiness and well-being are far more likely to result from attention to values that are intrinsic to us and that spending money on 'things' that have no meaning or deeper value is detrimental to our health.

Money matters; money pays for many valuable and meaningful things, the things that give our life purpose. Without enough money to pay for basic commodities it is much harder to flourish. Money matters because poverty is without question detrimental to health and well-being, but after we can afford to pay the bills money starts to represent the values that we live by.

How do you value money?

- Money enables me to buy what I want.
- Money allows me to do more with my life.
- Money allows me to care for those I love.

 **brilliant** recap

As we have seen in previous chapters, positive psychology is finding that research increasingly reveals that happiness and well-being are positively affected by being able to fulfil our needs and being free to do so.

This chapter has been examining the idea that who you are reflects what really matters to you and that you are more likely to flourish when you are living authentically and meaningfully:

● You have thought about what you value

● Where your values originate

● What you really care about

● You have explored your life purpose and who you are when you are truly authentic

● You have looked at how you value money and what it means to you.

This chapter has dug a little deeper into what those needs really are by exploring what you truly value and is meaningful to you. By knowing better who you really are you will begin to have much more purpose and direction in all aspects of your life.

The next chapter addresses the means by which you may find the self-discipline and self-regulation to really flourish.

CHAPTER 8

Getting wise: Developing your spiritual well-being

The wise man does not lay up treasure. The more he gives to others, the more he has for his own.

Lao-Tze, 600 BC Chinese philosopher and founder of Taoism

Being wise and having a spiritual dimension to your life are two different concepts, but both require self-knowledge integrated with an understanding of other people and a world view that accommodates ideas and values beyond yourself. Many spiritual practices and behaviours are the practices and behaviours of people who are living healthy, happy and fulfilled lives. Positive psychology, by examining what contributes to a flourishing life, is moving ever more closely into aspects of being that have traditionally been more the subject of philosophy. Time and again psychologists discover that, at the heart of a flourishing life, there lies the complex subject of a 'well-lived life'. Questions of morality, ethics and good character are found to be intricately linked to well-being, as is a sense of appreciation and compassion. Positive psychology, in examining what we mean by a flourishing life, also finds that it is often talking about 'wisdom'; findings of positive psychology seem to show that the happiest and most fulfilled people share many personality traits we recognise as the qualities of the wise or the spiritual.

The psychologist David Watson tells us that time and again studies in the field of positive psychology show that second to an active social life, 'people who describe themselves as "spiritual" or "religious" report higher levels of happiness than those who do not'.[151] This chapter will examine what the wise, spiritual and religious are doing and why it matters to your overall well-being.

Wisdom

Wisdom is generally considered to hold the best of human qualities and as such is an important subject of research into well-being. The psychology of wisdom-related knowledge understands wisdom as a combination of intellect, expertise and character. Positive psychology is showing more and more clearly that *character*, 'who we *are*', is one of the strongest contributing factors to a happy flourishing life. Character is also what separates intellect and cleverness from wisdom.

Wisdom is not intelligence but intelligence is an essential quality of the wise.

Wisdom involves the ability to assess knowledge in context and to be able to take account of other people at the same time as being able to balance long-term and short-term interests within existing and future environments. Basically wisdom involves an instinctive, as well as an experienced, balancing of factors that is able to go beyond a rule-based approach.

The psychologist Robert Sternberg believes that wisdom requires:

- *An awareness of your values.*
- *An effective management of conflicting interests, including self-management.*
- *an ability to gain insight into the subtleties of a particular situation and to use this insight for developing a useful strategy.* [152]

Positive psychologists list the following qualities of someone recognised as wise:

- Able to be comfortable with both the certainty and uncertainty in complex situations.

- Sees the process as more important than the outcome, while still seeking to achieve the best outcome.

- Can hold to their principles and purpose while utilising their knowledge and expertise in the service of others and the environment.

brilliant example

Barry Schwartz gives us a great example of how much we neglect to ask for wisdom as a skill, yet how it can make all the difference. He uses the example of the duties listed in the job specification of a hospital janitor. The skills required cover several pages, yet don't speak of any social or interpersonal skills. When experienced janitors are questioned about their job, it is immediately apparent that the best janitors are constantly modifying their work in order to take account of other people, for example not intruding on family grief, re-mopping a floor without complaint because it soothed and calmed a patient and generally being aware of the needs of the people and patients around them. The wisest janitors combine human skills with job experience, such that they can assess when to bend the rules and have the character to do so. The janitors who behave in this way affect the recovery period of patients and are also the happiest in their work, yet such skills are not 'required' for the job.[153]

Many of the skills shown in the wise are similar to those required for high emotional intelligence, but with the added aspect of experience, expertise and knowledge, in service to situations and others beyond oneself.

Based on cultural and historical analysis, facets of wisdom include being able to address difficult problems regarding the meaning and conduct of life; promotes growth in individuals and society; combines knowledge with character and knows the limits of knowledge. These characteristics may be hard to achieve but according to psychologist Paul Baltes are easily and universally recognised.[154]

 brilliant definition

Wisdom includes:

- High levels of thinking
- High level of interest in others
- A deep understanding of people and their problems – incorporates others' values, respectful of others' needs
- Fairness
- The acceptance of others' opinions and ideas
- An awareness that we continue to learn from others
- Reflection, understated and quiet
- Insightfullness
- Listening accurately
- Admitting to being wrong and making mistakes
- Knowing that knowledge can be wrong, and allows doubt and acceptance for what is not known
- Ability to problem solve
- Being sensible and balanced
- Humility.

Wisdom is not:

● Knowing the answer

● Being right

● Always the same

● Cleverness

● Facts

● Advice.

Is age a factor?

Wisdom grows with age and experience, but being older or experienced does not necessarily mean you are wise! The research in this area is mixed. Expertise and experience are attributes of the wise, so it is understandable that age might be a factor as we gain more experience and expertise over time; however, the research is inconclusive, which would indicate the effect of character – and character is not the sole prerogative of the old. As we go through life we get more opportunity to expand our knowledge; those who become insightful and are able to grow out of adversity are more likely to be 'wise'. Gaining general wisdom is easier than gaining personal wisdom, as judgement of other people's actions requires less strength of character than learning insight and emotional maturity in ourselves. Wisdom that builds internal mastery is more dependent on personal growth and insight.[155] Most psychologists believe that it is personal wisdom that grows with age. Personal wisdom requires attention to self-discovery, knowing what you value, learning to control your emotions and positive reflection.

How to develop wisdom:

- Develop your emotional intelligence

- Strengthen your ability to problem solve

- Build your resilience and develop the ability to cope

- Become more self-aware and self-accepting

- Slow down and become more present

- Understand and forgive more

- Learn and grow

- Be generous and philanthropic in outlook

- Be grateful

- Know what you believe and value and respect others' beliefs and values.

Expertise and experience

Wisdom requires the need for some kind of expertise or intellect; we need tools to work with, knowledge and mastery of some kind. However, it is *how* we use our knowledge and expertise that is the source of our wisdom. Without knowledge or expertise some successful actions and behaviour may be instinctive or lucky but not wise. For instance, as Aristotle tells us, real bravery is an assessment of risk followed by action. Action that takes no account of the risk is merely foolhardy. An *expert* fisherman can almost smell where the fish are or turn for home ahead of the weather. A *wise* fisherman also knows who to have in his boat and how to get the best out of his crew, his boat and the sea, while also teaching his craft, building relationships and keeping order. His experience and expertise are crucial to his decisions, as are the times he has failed, reflected and learnt in order to build that expertise.

- What is your greatest expertise?
- What do you know really well?

More importantly, do you have the courage and confidence in *yourself* as much as in your talents and knowledge? If the answer to this is no, why is this? Check out the facts and remember: **everything you do affects everything you do.** Do not be afraid to reflect and learn about yourself in the same way you learn all skills and expertise.

Having a mentor

Research shows that wisdom requires nurturing from outside as well as within: having the support of a mentor or guide, someone we respect for their opinions and abilities from whom we can learn, and who will help us evaluate and mediate our own actions. Education that teaches the young to think rather than just to focus on accumulating facts is the start of encouraging wisdom in the young. Many great leaders and successful people will speak of the effect a teacher or role model had in shaping their life. Having someone wise in your life is an essential part of developing all your strengths and talents as well as wisdom and is a lifelong necessity. When you say things out loud to someone else, when you explain your thinking to someone else whom you trust, you hear yourself better. In a professional capacity this is how you develop skills and expertise under the guidance of an expert and 'life' is no different.

- Are you able to share your problems or do you prefer to work things out alone?
- When did you last share a problem?
- Who has been or is a mentor or guide in your life?
- What did your parents teach you? Are you wise as a parent?
- Do you have a hero, someone you would be if you could?

What advice would they give you about your life right now? When do you show the same qualities and strengths you respect them for?

Learning from mistakes

The wise are not afraid of failing, changing their minds or not knowing.[156] Rather they are more likely to be acutely aware of how little they do know. Having a growth mindset is an essential quality to wisdom. Can you see your mistakes as opportunities to learn or do you see them as failure? When did you last change your mind?

Growing and developing are not all we take from our mistakes; our mistakes are also the best way we discover how to do things well. A friend of mine trained as a health visitor and she was expert in her knowledge, until she had four children of her own and put all the expertise she had learned – technically – to the test for herself. She is now a much wiser health visitor; she changed her mind and even now, with all her experience, is still open to what she doesn't know, much more than in her 'clever' youth.

- Think of a really big mistake you are now grateful for having made.

Develop your curiosity

Wisdom requires that we be curious. Develop your growth mindset by opening yourself to different ideas and viewpoints. It is impossible to learn anything without curiosity. The wise are not afraid to look stupid.

 **exercise**

● Spend more time today asking questions than looking for answers.

● Really listen, be curious and if you don't understand something someone is telling you, be more curious. Put your watch on the other arm to remind you that you are having a curious day.

Curiosity:

● Opens us up to opportunities

● Helps us understand other people

● Allows insight and new perspectives

● Builds knowledge, both of what we know and what we don't know.

Humility and self-acceptance

Humility contains many of the qualities that are those of the wise, most especially total self-acceptence and interest in others. Humility is not false modesty. According to psychologist June Price Tangney, humility is an accurate assessment of your strengths and weaknesses, such that you know what you do and don't know. It also involves the idea of bringing this knowledge of yourself to the service of the bigger picture, being open to new ideas and understanding the differences and needs in others. Having humility holds the ability to move beyond oneself, becoming 'unselved' such that attention and need are shifted outwards with an increased interest in others without negating oneself.[157] Humility is the opposite of narcissism.

When wise leaders display this quality, they show it by being able to hold a perspective of their role while focusing on the unique qualities and potential in others.

Self-acceptence is a running theme in positive psychology; knowing yourself, being comfortable with **all** that you are enable you to 'get over yourself'.

Listening

You can't be wise if you don't listen. How well do you really listen? We all think we listen; it is so simple we don't stop to notice. Listening well is the most important skill in my profession as a coach and I am still learning the art.

Have you ever had the experience of driving a familiar route and getting to a destination with the feeling that you were hardly aware of the route you took? You can be in this half-awake mode in much of your life and you can have whole conversations with people where you are hardly there. Try listening with your full attention and you will be amazed at how much more you hear.

Develop your imagination

Being able to imagine both intellectually and emotionally, to be empathetic to the needs and perspectives of other people, are a necessary quality of wisdom. The psychologists Ute Kunzman and Paul Baltes tell us that, 'an advice giver who is not able to imagine how a needy person feels, is unlikely to make the effort to engage in wisdom related knowledge'.[158] To have the ability to imagine and inhabit other cultural and complex situations is a fundamental requirement of wisdom-related characteristics.

Use your imagination to support your curiosity and to broaden your perception. Try imagining what being someone else would be like. Wisdom involves being able to take account of other people's perspectives, viewpoints and value structures.

- What would it be like to see the world from a different religious or political perspective?
- What would it be like to be your hero for a day?
- What would it be like to live on a pound a day?
- What would it be like to say what you really believe, and who would you say it to?
- What would it be like to know you had only a year to live?
- What would you do if money were no object?

Use your imagination as a tool to inhabit worlds and experiences that are not yours.

Time for reflection and evaluation

I discovered some years ago that many barristers were using psychoanalysts, not because they needed psychoanalysis but because it gave them an hour a week to be structurally self-accountable. Nowadays top leaders often use coaches for the same reason. Making time for reflection and assessment of your life, in all its guises, matters. Recently I did some research into the effect of one and a half hours a week of group life coaching on well-being and happiness – a workshop designed as time to reflect and focus in a structured way on all aspects of your life. My research found that people were happier and felt better for active structured reflection, compared with people who just met for a chat about life.[159] Just rushing ever forward stops us from assessing the choices we are making and, more importantly, the choices we might make if we stopped to reflect, learn and dare to learn more. Wise people have a reflective attitude.[160]

Awareness of others

How much are you lost in your own world? It is easy, especially when we are busy and distracted, to become wrapped up in our own concerns. We touched on how looking out for someone else is a great coping strategy in adversity but being aware of other people also builds your knowledge and experience of life as much as learning about who you are. One of the top characteristics associated with wisdom is concern for others.[161]

 **exercise**

● Notice how the next person you talk to is feeling. How are they dressed, how do they sound, how do they look?

● Next, try just being with someone without thinking or analysing. Just be with them, without any judgement, just experience them in all that they are.

● What is the difference between these two ways of being with someone? And what did you notice, if anything, about yourself during this exercise?

Developing your spirituality

Being spiritual in psychological and scientific terms refers to an aspect of being in the world, rather than esoteric experiences with ghosts and spirits. A spiritual person is someone who believes they are a part of something greater than themselves, who has a reverence and awe for the world around them, and finds meaning from an understanding of the world and their place in it that transcends human existence. Those who have a spiritual or a religious practice are among the happiest, healthiest people[162] and it appears not to matter if the practice and belief are formally religious or with no belief in God or a deity. What affects well-being is the capacity to find the sacred in everyday events, to be appreciative and grateful, and connected positively to other people. Being spiritual is not the same as being religious and we will first look at the advantages to well-being from having a religious belief and then we will examine positive spiritual practices.

The advantages of religious belief and practice

Religious people practise a spiritual interpretation of the world that is organised, rule-based and part of a cohesive belief structure, which is usually based on a deity or God. Actively religious people have a meaningful story and framework for their lives. They also belong to a community of people who have the same meaning and interpretation of life and their role in it; a community with whom to share birth and death, joy and suffering. Religiousness fills many human needs. Religion not only gives life meaning, but religious people know they matter – to God – and have hope, all of which are important aspects to health and well-being.

 insight

People who are actively religious are:

- Less likely to be delinquent
- Less likely to abuse drugs and alcohol
- Less likely to divorce
- Less likely to commit suicide
- More likely to live longer
- More likely to retain or recover greater happiness after bereavement, divorce, unemployment or ill health
- Twice as likely to say they are 'very happy'.[163]

Research shows that being religious is one of the most consistent components to positively affect well-being and happiness. Most of the research comes from America where religious practice is synonymous with the social and emotional support of belonging to a church. Having a guide and rules by which to live reduces people's moral choices, and less choice makes us happier. The research into being religious highlights some of the anomalies involved with thinking it is possible to prescribe well-being. Religious people are more likely to be conservative in their moral values rather than liberal, and as conservatives they are more likely to have a fixed rather than a growth mindset. How does this fit with the research that autonomy and having an open mindset are also important positive attributes to happiness and well-being? Nothing is straightforward and the deeper one goes into exploring all the common factors of a healthy happy fulfilled life, the more questions of morality, character and social responsibility come to the fore.

Like being in the army, the advantages of having fewer choices, close social support, a sense of purpose, self-regulation and commitment are all positive factors for a happy life. Add to that the advantage of reflection and a philosophy of appreciation and generosity, and it is hardly surprising that religious belief and practice are so positively beneficial, despite some anomalies.

The fact is that religious and spiritual practices are as different and as varied as our own personal values. There is a world of difference between a Calvinistic Protestant interpretation of the bible and that of a Franciscan monk. Most Muslims do not interpret the Qur'an in the same way as the Taliban. Similarly, some new-age interpretations of native spirituality are not the same practices as those of true native American shamans. What is universal is that in practising and following the discipline of a religious belief people are afforded both structure and support. They are also challenged to develop and seek self-knowledge and self-discipline. All religious spiritual practices require self-regulation and an acceptance of authority, however all religions can be interpreted either fundamentally or mystically. We live in an age where we can explore other religious practices as never before, and positive psychology is showing us just how important many of these practices are. The Dalai Lama and Desmond Tutu, two men who are always laughing and smiling despite living through the horrific and terrible suffering of their people, are shining examples of the positive effect that living a religious life affords.

Spiritual well-being

Well-being that is derived from having a spiritual outlook and practice is derived from an active and practical way of being in the world. Being 'spiritual' does not mean believing that you know all the answers to life and the universe. The more insightful and truly spiritual people are much more likely to have a deep humility and respect for all others while holding themselves accountable and responsible. For the positive psychologist Kenneth Pargament, spirituality is the 'search for the sacred'. It is an ongoing process.[164]

All knowledge appears to carry with it a danger of superiority – think of academics, government officials, mothers, teenagers who have lost their virginity – and spirituality is no exception. I have come across people who wear their 'spirituality' like a trophy that sets them apart from those lesser mortals who haven't got it yet. Marilyn Williamson was once asked why she tolerated fundamentalist Christians; her reply was to ask in return what her 'spiritual' questioner's problem was with fundamentalist Christians. The response was 'They're so judgemental'! The kind of spiritual belief and practice that positive psychology is finding supports a flourishing healthy life is much more about practice and behaviour rather than spiritual interpretations or esoteric knowledge.

Spiritual people are:

- Insightful
- Understanding
- Have perspective
- Optimistic

- Accepting
- Grateful
- Humble and aware of the complexity of things
- Loving
- Forgiving
- Aware of being part of something greater than themselves
- Compassionate and empathetic of the needs of others
- Hold to a self-regulatory practice.

brilliant tip

You are more likely to achieve goals that are sacred to you. Things that are sacred are also most meaningful to us.[165]

Spiritual practices that support well-being

Be present

Being open to the present and being attentive is at the heart of ALL spiritual practices; concentration on the present moment is a recurring theme. In Chapter 3 we covered the art of savouring, a wonderful way to be pleasurably present. Being open to the present also allows you to see opportunities and to be better able to rise to all the possibilities that each moment presents. Being open to the present involves being open to events as they occur and to work with things as they **are**. Sometimes things don't go according to plan, but if you are open to the present you are better able to accept and perhaps gain from the unexpected.

Being fully present is important because it causes you to:

● Slow down

● Become more aware

● Notice emotion

● Regulate emotion

● Appreciate what is present right now

● Feel wonder and awe

● Feel compassion

● See and hear more.

brilliant exercise

Just for today, let go of any investment you have in the outcome of your actions. You can still focus on the outcome you would like and act accordingly, but attend more to being present to your immediate actions and choices. Invest in the process, notice and be aware of others' needs and values, and try incorporating someone else's needs in your choice of action as well as your own principles and purpose.

Practise self-awareness

You can practise self-awareness by noticing your thinking or by noticing your body.

brilliant tip

To bring yourself to awareness of your body, sit with your eyes closed and lift your arm as slowly as you possibly can. Bring all your focus and attention to the arm and the muscles employed to

> the service of moving it. Or you can notice yourself walking. See how slowly and smoothly you can walk, become fully aware of each movement as you lift and move each leg. Or just focus on your breathing.
>
> All these exercises can be done during the day and will sharpen your focus both to yourself and to your surroundings.

Practising gratitude

We have already seen that being grateful is one of the greatest attributes of a flourishing, fulfilled and happy life. Gratitude is a core ingredient in both spiritual and religious practice and may account on its own for much of the well-being factors attributable to spiritual practice.

Spiritual and religious people show much more gratitude in their daily lives.[166]

Share your gratitude with your friends, family and work colleagues. Find time to share what you enjoy and like about someone. Be appropriate – keep the smoochy exchanges for those closest to you. I have just received an encouraging card from a friend saying she wanted to give me the strength I have given her. I feel both thanked and supported and am so grateful to have such a supportive friend. Looking for what you love and enjoy in other people, telling them why you are grateful for them being in your life or thanking someone personally with a card or e-mail after a meal or gift is not just a polite habit, but a valuable habit. Keep it genuine.

How can your gratitude become more sacred? As you start to acknowledge what you are grateful for you will find yourself beginning to become more attentive; as you become more attentive you start to notice more; as you notice more you become more aware of how wonderful things are and you become even more grateful for the real abundance in your life.

 Grace is the awareness that we have not earned, nor do we deserve, what we have been given.

Gregg Kretch

See the wonder around you

Deep gratitude can inspire awe. Awe contains sensitivity to greatness or being part of something bigger and greater than oneself. Awe is similar to the emotion felt during peak experience or flow. Awe is an emotional response similar to wonder and reverence; it can be both a spiritual response as well as heightened joy and wonder in response to greatness. For the psychologist Bulkeley, wonder contains two effects: 1) the self is shaken (decentred) by an experience that is powerful, unexpected and new; 2) the self is remade (recentred) in response to new knowledge and understanding.[167]

Both wonder and awe are intense emotions that have the capacity to open our hearts.

- When did you last feel a sense of awe and wonder?
- Open your heart. What is stopping you from opening your heart?
- Open your heart to the beauty in others.
- Open your heart to all the abundance in your life.

Practise forgiveness

Forgiveness is a daily and sometimes hourly activity. Sometimes it is not possible to forgive and forget but it is possible to choose to let go of holding onto pain that someone else is causing you. You *can* choose how much you allow someone else to affect your happiness. Forgiveness is a complicated process and this book cannot do more than remind you that it is a spiritual practice and offer some research. The more you apply what works for you from other chapters in this book, the more likely you are to come across the key to the cupboard in the emotional room that will free your heart to forgive.

⚐ brilliant insight

Research has shown that grieving men who were able to forgive a woman aborting their baby were less likely to suffer depression,[168] and women who were able to forgive fathers who abused them were less anxious than those who did not.[169]

Studies in forgiveness have shown that people experience:

- Less depression
- Less anger
- Less unhappiness.

Studies have also shown that people who have been forgiven or imagine being forgiven experience less guilt, anger and sadness and are also more hopeful and grateful.[170]

Start by forgiving yourself. Do you need to forgive yourself, and what would you like to be forgiven for? Is there something in your life that if you put it right would be a weight off your back?

✳ brilliant tip

If there is anything that you need to atone for, decide to do it and tell someone that this is your intention. If what you wish to atone for is secret, there is a great website called www.postsecret.com where you can send a postcard with your secret on it anonymously.

Forgiveness is a huge subject; the emotions involved in forgiving someone for being late are quite different from forgiving
a drunk driver who has killed your child. The mother of one of
the victims of the July 2002 London bomb gave up her profession as a priest; she said that she could not preach on the
subject of forgiveness, the cornerstone of a Christian life, if
she herself could not forgive. People can and do forgive such
things. The father of Marie Wilson killed by an IRA bomb did,
and the rest of his life was spent in service to building peace in
Northern Ireland. The bigger the commitment and depth of
forgiving, the greater is the effect on well-being. Forgiving a
partner has a far greater impact on your well-being than forgiving someone with whom you don't have a relationship.[171]
Learning how to forgive is a process, and as the rewards are
felt the process develops. If you have something of some
magnitude that you cannot forgive, start by forgiving only what
you can; start by forgiving yourself for being unable to forgive
– today, for an hour. Letting go of your emotional attachment
is another way to begin. This book and positive psychology
can do no more than tell you that forgiveness is a gift you give
to yourself; your well-being is in your hands and one can only
be amazed and inspired by people who find the strength to do
so.

Practise self-acceptance

A great way to self-acceptance is to celebrate all you are. If your
heart could celebrate some part of you, what would it be? If
your heart could accept your weakness, what would it be? We
began this book with self-acceptance. I hope you are happy
and content with who you are. Revisit Chapters 1 and 2 for a
reminder.

 exercise

Notice when you are at odds with yourself and when you feel strong emotion towards someone else. This emotion is an indication that there is a part of you that isn't seen. Hiding bits of you away, the bits you think are bad or not allowed, suppressing what you judge to be 'wrong' with yourself are great ways to fuel these negative emotions but are also unauthentic. Examine what is behind strong emotions, find the icebergs mentioned in Chapter 6 and if there is stuff to deal with, deal with it, by changing your story, changing your response or practising forgiveness.

● Do your values honour yourself in a healthy way?

● Use your strengths to practice self-acceptance.

● If there is something you have done that you feel was bad do you:

a) Feel you are a bad person. or

b) Feel what you did was a bad thing?

If you answered yes to (a) you are less likely to repair either your behaviour or to put the wrong right. In fact, you may even run from the issue or become defensive rather than face up to what you have done. If you answered yes to (b) you are more likely to be sorry and try to understand what caused you to act in this manner. Remember that keeping things specific and temporary rather than general or personal is important. If your thinking is more inclined to be (a), take time to examine and try to understand your actions, learn so that in future your behaviour might be different, seek forgiveness and move on. If you are just feeling bad or worthless you are less likely to examine and put right why you did what you did, and self-acceptance is best served by getting curious and active about your behaviour. It is harder to accept yourself if you don't think you can change. Knowing you *can* change and you are the master of your behaviour is fundamental to self-acceptance.

Practise self-regulation

Spiritual practice of any kind requires that you regulate yourself to some extent, setting aside time in the day for contemplation, or regulating your behaviour in adherence to what you value and in service to the needs of others. Regulating your thoughts as well as your emotions and actions is a central component of religious and spiritual practice.

Self-regulation of some kind is good for more than your spiritual well-being. In a study by the psychologist Roy Baumiester, people who were given self-regulatory exercises such as practising sitting up straighter, watching what they ate, keeping on top of their finances or keeping to a regular exercise programme were better able to complete performance tasks than people who had not practised self-regulation. The harder the self-regulators had worked on their exercises, the better they did in the task.[172]

Self-regulation has a marked effect on your mental ability as well as improving your ability to regulate yourself in other areas of your life: the more you practise regulating your behaviour in some way, the better other parts of your life get.

Practise compassion

All spiritual practice involves compassion. Compassion involves reaching out to others with warmth and no desire other than for good things for them. The Dalai Lama describes compassion as *'A mental attitude based on the wish for others to be free of their suffering and is associated with a sense of commitment, responsibility and respect towards others'.*[173] Compassion is not sympathy; it holds a force in our hearts that calls us to action. Sympathy and empathy are important ingredients but compassion has an open heart to another's plight. To be truly compassionate means being able to imagine how someone else is feeling and then to act from there. Compassion starts when you focus on someone else.

- What suffering in others moves you?
- What do you feel compelled to help and support?
- To whom do you feel most compassion?
- How much compassion do you feel for yourself?

brilliant tip

Do not pity people or yourself; pity is poison. Sympathy and compassion, however, are great soul food.

Practise mindfulness

Earlier in this chapter we touched on mindfulness as a way to open awareness of ourselves and other people, and in Chapter 3 we saw the benefits of savouring. Mindfulness is not just at the heart of developing your spiritual awareness, but enhances every aspect of well-being.

Mindfulness positively affects:

- Memory
- Reduces stress
- Improves competence
- Better health
- Creativity.

Mindfulness

Being mindful is the opposite of being mindless. When you are mindful you are really awake to everything and fully present to the multifaceted world around you and the many different possible perspectives, not through being analytical or judging the world around you but by being so awake and open that the newness in each moment is experienced fully, consciously and self-consciously. It is interesting to note that being mindful includes many of the factors already understood as being vital to well-being. Good mindfulness becomes better with practice!

 **definition**

The qualities of mindfulness

- Being non-judgemental, just observing what is. Being fully present, accepting things as they are
- Being in the process not the outcome, not striving to an objective
- Feeling patient and respectful, knowing things will happen as they will
- Trusting in yourself and your abilities, and life
- Seeing anew, having an open mindset, seeing novelty and uncertainty
- Being considerate to all around you
- Letting go, noticing context, thought and emotions but letting them pass
- Able to change and adapt to meet circumstance and situations
- Loving and kind, compassionate and forgiving
- Empathetic and aware of the needs of others and other perspectives
- Appreciative, reverent and grateful, for all that is right now
- Generous without need of reciprocity.[174]

Mindlessness is:

- A fixed mindset
- Accept things without question
- Habitual
- Oblivious to context, one-dimensional
- Unobservant
- Certain, blind
- Rigid
- Barely aware of yourself or others
- Focused on results.

brilliant example

Being mindful lessens regret

Psychologists Langer, Macatonis and Golub tested the effects of being mindful on future regret. Participants were told that they were going to get an opportunity to gamble, with the chance of winning $100 with no risk to themselves. Those participants who were told to 'be aware of what they are thinking and feeling' while waiting to be called felt the least regret after being told that they had missed the opportunity after failing to see the light calling them. They were also told how much money the people who hadn't missed it had won. Other participants were instructed to do nothing or watch *Seinfeld* or a film on the Civil War.[175]

Meditation

I have always thought meditation to be a good thing. However, since studying all the research into health and well-being I now see meditation as being as important to our health and well-being as drinking water and exercising. Meditation is a cornerstone of spiritual practice. Any exercise that quietens the mind is wonderful for our well-being, health and happiness. If you can discipline yourself to build a mindful or meditative practice as a regular habit, your whole life will benefit.

Meditation has been shown to relieve:

- Chronic pain
- Anxiety and panic disorder
- Dermatalogical disorders
- Depression
- Stress.

Meditation has been shown to support:

- Self-actualisation, personal growth and self-esteem
- Memory and intelligence
- Creativity
- Happiness
- Empathy
- A sense of control and autonomy
- Improved reaction time
- Better concentration.

Meditation is correlated with many aspects of being alert and also has a positive hormonal effect that is similar to taking exercise. Meditation is good for your health, your mind, your abilities **and** your happiness. When you meditate you feel great! What is stopping you?

Meditation starts with being mindful and attentive. All the practices in this chapter will bring your attention to being more open to the present in a way that requires some discipline and practice. For a fully flourishing life it is not required that you tune out and sit Zen-like, observing. Rather you are able to function in control of your emotions and desires through self-knowledge, understanding of other people and wisdom. Religious or spiritual practices encourage your humanity and transcendence. Openness and being present brings abundance in opportunity and experience that is much greater than just rushing through life chasing blindly after one objective or another. Gandhi was said to meditate for two hours a day. When he had problems he apparently meditated for four hours and when things got really bad he meditated for eight hours! Positive psychology is not suggesting such extremes, but all the behaviours and practices of this chapter are powerful ingredients in *how* you live your life spiritually and wisely.

 **brilliant** recap

This chapter has looked at the qualities of the wise, that to be wise:

- You need knowledge and expertise.
- You are able to imagine and empathise with the experience of others.
- You are happy to learn from mistakes and are curious and open to uncertainty.
- You know your strengths, weaknesses and values and respect the needs and values of others.
- You use this knowledge in service to other people.

We looked at the advantages of a spiritual or religious belief and noted that people who have a religious or spiritual practice are more likely to be very happy than those who do not.

We examined a number of emotions and practices that research reveals spiritual people share:

- Being fully present
- Being self-aware

- Feeling grateful
- Feeling wonder and awe
- Being forgiving
- Self-accepting
- Self-regulating
- Compassionate
- Mindful
- Meditating.

CHAPTER 9

Positive health: How to build physical well-being and live longer

A sound mind in a sound body is a short but full description of a happy state in this world.

John Locke, 1632–1704

Remember in Chapter 3 Robert Emmons's research that boosted people's happiness after they kept a gratitude journal for three weeks. Not only did these people get happier but they slept better and spent more time exercising. They also reported fewer physical symptoms, such as pain. The happier you get, the healthier you get – because the happier you are, the better care you take of yourself and others.

Much of this book has been focusing on the effect that the emotions have on our minds and the best ways to get our minds to embrace and use our emotions, as knowledge and motivation and in order to cope better. Emotions also have a powerful effect on our bodies. Emotions are activated through the endocrine system and are a vital part of the way we function physically.

The famous research conducted by the behavioural psychologist Skinner demonstrated how our physical responses can be triggered by mental stimulation. Every time a dog was fed, a bell was rung and eventually the dog would salivate at the sound of a bell. Primary school physics teaches us the wonderful physical responses our body makes when flooded with adrenaline in a fearful situation. And where would we be if there was no physical response to the mental delight a man experiences at the thought of a beautiful naked woman (or some of the stranger thoughts or images that can activate the sex organs)? Saliva, sweating and sexual excitement are very basic physical responses to thoughts and emotions, and researchers are increasingly able to tell us what effect our thoughts and behaviours have on our neuro-endocrine system. Research is becoming much less subjective when it can prove that we are physically better off not just when we eat and exercise but when we think in particular ways by understanding and testing both neurological and hormonal connections. Science can tell us that responses are shaped in early childhood, and our genetic bias, as we have already noted, determines a great deal. However, the research is also showing that although our minds have a huge effect on our emotional responses, we also know much more about how important the effect of physical activity is on both our cognitive skills and our emotions. Our mind is our body and the old adage 'A healthy mind needs a healthy body' is a physical reality, but it is also the case that a healthy body needs a healthy mind. We think better when we are healthy and fit and we are healthier and fitter when we think better.

↗ brilliant insight

Happiness affects our health more than our health affects our happiness. A very famous study showed that 80 per cent of people felt their life to be average or above average after becoming paraplegics.[176] Perhaps those who recover their previous happiness after some physical adversity are able to do so because they become more grateful and appreciative for the life they *do* have.

And being physically well affects mental heath. Being mentally well is very positively affected by being physically well; in fact, exercise is now considered to be the best cure for most cases of depression.[177] Severe clinical depression can also be regulated better with exercise as well as medication. Several recent studies have shown that there is a positive relationship between exercise and subjective well-being,[178] and it is also the case that the more active you are, the less likely you are to suffer anxiety and stress.

Physical well-being

The first thing you can do to improve your physical well-being is to notice your posture and how you are breathing. Breath is life and if you can do nothing else, relax and drop your shoulders, straighten up and breathe deeply. Let your stomach stretch with each intake of breath through the nose and let the air out slowly through your mouth. Stretch your neck muscles, roll your head, and if you are sitting for long periods at a desk or computer, invest in a good chair and remember to get up and stretch yourself at regular intervals.

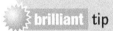 **tip**

Doing regular exercise positively affects your cognitive ability.

The importance of exercise

From childhood to old age, regular exercise improves memory, planning, organisation and concentration. In old age, regular exercise reduces mental as well as physical decline and in primary school children improves exam results. By exercising we are stimulating the flow of oxygen to the brain and it is also thought to stimulate the growth of new brain cells.[179] Research into exercise and depression is well known but it cannot be repeated too often. Exercise is better than pills in curing depression and even when pills are required, pills and exercise affect the likelihood of recurrence better than medication only.

Exercising is essential to your health and well-being; this is well known and yet it seems that knowing something and doing something are very different beasts. If you have struggled with good intentions but your exercise habit is still failing you, here are a few tips.

Exercise with other people

We have already noted that the very happiest people are the ones with an active social life. Just going for a walk with a friend is a great way to start getting some exercise. Choosing an exercise routine that involves other people is a booster to your well-being on both scores. Taking up a team sport also gives you the opportunity for getting some flow in your life, as does dancing.

brilliant tip

Commit to an exercise routine that would let others down if you missed it.

Walking facts

Walking 1 mile in 15 minutes burns as many calories as running the same distance in 8.3 minutes.

Walking 2 miles a day, three days a week reduces weight by 1lb every three weeks.

Every minute you walk adds 1.3–.2 minutes to your life.[180]

Fun ways to get physical and off the sofa:

- Go dancing
- Play a team sport
- Walk and talk
- Bell ringing
- Get a dog
- Geocaching with the children
- Have sex.

Keep it fun and moderate. Be careful of being too competitive, as there is evidence to show that exercising in a competitive environment doesn't make you feel as good as exercising in a fun way.

Physical well-being affects everything!

 tip

Imagine you are already fit doing your normal day-to-day work.

brilliant example

One group of hotel cleaners were told that the work they did was perfect exercise for cardiac fitness and well-being. After four weeks they were fitter in several ways compared to hotel cleaners who had not been told that their work benefited their fitness.[181]

Good ways to get going and stay going:

- Get an exercise buddy and commit to only four weeks to start with, and celebrate completing a four-week programme before starting another.
- If you go to a gym, how can getting there be more fun?
- Use your strengths to make an exercise programme.
- Park further away from the office.
- Imagine every morning when you wake up that you are already fit and be grateful for the physical ability of your wonderful body!

Positive eating and drinking

We don't really need positive psychologists to tell us that feeling good is affected by what we put in our bodies as much as what we do with them. You are a plant; the statement 'You are what you eat' is simple and true. How come we find it so difficult to moderate what we put into our bodies? This is not a diet book but we can use some positive psychology to help us.

Remember the lemon barley sweet? The more you tell yourself not to think about something, the greater your response becomes. This is part of what happens when we obsess over the shape of our bodies and food.

Research shows that we are living longer and healthier but in the developed world we are also getting fatter and suffering from more diabetes, coronary disease and cancer than ever before. The effects of an unhealthy lifestyle are so well known and yet we continue to eat and drink unhealthily. So much unhappiness is connected to our bodies that there is obviously much more to it.

Healthy drinking

Drink more water; it helps flush out toxins and fills us up. The positive effects of drinking more water are now so accepted that primary school children are told to take a bottle of water to school with them, because research has shown that if we drink more water our cognitive skills improve. Decide, from today, to drink more water. This will affect your body and your mind.

brilliant tip

Keep a glass of water either by the kitchen sink or by the basin in the bathroom. Each time you visit either the kitchen or the bathroom, drink it and refill the glass.

Watch your alcohol. One glass a night is fine, drinking that glass with food is better and drinking in moderation with other people over a meal is the healthiest way to consume alcohol. Alcohol drunk this way in moderation is actually good for you. Research has shown that moderate drinkers suffer less depression than teetotalers![182]

Drinking is most harmful to your health when you binge drink or allow your consumption to go beyond 21 units a week for a man and 14 units a week for a woman. People who drink excessively suffer depression, anxiety, dementia and liver damage. Count how much money you spend on alcohol a week and imagine that every pound spent over the recommended limit is buying you less life. If you do binge drink, what does this experience give you? Can you imagine having this experience another way? What are you valuing?

brilliant tip

Drink a glass of water before and after you drink a glass of alcohol.

Caffeine in any form is also best drunk in moderation, so choose to have a herb tea instead of coffee or tea sometimes.

Health and a positive relationship with food

A young man on his gap year teaching in India was struggling to connect to the children on his first day. As he groped for a subject, he asked 'Who likes food?' The class erupted with excitement and he thought he'd cracked it. His next question, 'What is your favourite food?', completely baffled them. We have so much food and choice of types of food in the West that we have lost any concept of food as something that keeps us alive. There are unending amounts of research and information on what foods are real health, happiness and energy boosters. All food is good for you in moderation and too much worry about what you are or are not eating could make you unhappy. You may get all the information and spend hours buying all the right things but the process of doing this can be stressful and all the benefit of eating the right stuff will be lost. Food is a pleasure and preparing food is a wonderful way to be mindful and present. Eating with other people is the best way to savour both food and company.

There have been literally hundreds of studies into the effects of high and low cholesterol, so much so that some long-term studies threw up a statistic that those with the highest cholesterol actually lived longer than those with the supposedly healthier low cholesterol. There has since been debate over why and what the connection is of low cholesterol to infection, violent death and suicide.[183] Some studies have suggested that you live longest with high cholesterol because you suffer less infection, depression and cancer; on the other hand, high cholesterol is also a health hazard for your heart and the official advice is still to lower your cholesterol. What the true risks are can never be fully ascertained and most research can only show a trend with large numbers. We can become overloaded with research on the subject of what we should and should not put in our bodies but there are a few givens.

Recommendations for good eating habits:

- Eat fruit and vegetables daily.
- Make time to cook; cooking your own food is healthier not just because the ingredients are better but the time you spend preparing it can be mindful or social.
- Eat more slowly and relish your food (remember how important savouring is).
- Eat what you enjoy; keep portions moderate, remember self-regulation, but don't deny yourself the pleasure of eating.
- Eat with someone else.
- Eat better snacks; nuts, dried fruit or home-made pop corn.

- Have regular meal times.
- Don't see food as a problem, see it as the source of life that it is.

Why not give your body a good cleanout now and then? Fasting every once in a while is very good for clearing your system both physically and mentally and is still used as a spiritual practice.

brilliant tip

Have a monthly detox for a day. Drink only water, either hot or cold, with a slice of lemon, and eat only fruit, vegetables and pulses. Cut out alcohol, caffeine, all dairy products, sugar, wheat and meat.

Love your body

Love your body more than food. When did you last stand naked in front of a mirror and really look at yourself? I am old enough for this to be much harder than it was 20 years ago. We live in a youth-obsessed culture and as we get older we can be made to feel that the natural changes to our bodies should somehow be overcome, hidden and even denied. The sexiest people are all shapes, sizes and ages – what they share is confidence and delight in physical expression. Really sexy people are at ease with their bodies. Happy people appreciate and value their bodies.

Everybody has flaws and imperfections. If you focus on your physical flaws rather than seeing what is beautiful about yourself, you will stop enjoying your full physical potential. Eating and body image can become so distorted that pleasure in a body that can run, jump and dance is lost along with the pleasure of eating. If you are young, be grateful for your body now. In 20 or 30 years you will long to have it again.

How what we focus on becomes visibly and metaphorically bigger

Children were asked to draw Father Christmases in September, October, November, December, just before Christmas and in January. The Father Christmases got bigger the closer to Christmas it got and also his bag of presents got much bigger just before Christmas. In January they were small again.[184] This is a great piece of research that demonstrates how the importance of something becomes bigger when it is everywhere and becomes the focus of our thoughts and attention. We do this in the same way when food becomes an issue for us. Counting calories, obsessing about how much we weigh. Thinking constantly about our physical selves in terms of food and weight distort our relationship both with our bodies (which *are* beautiful) and with food. If we are constantly either denying or obsessing about food we are like the children just before Christmas and there is no room left in our drawing for all the joys and wonders and other pleasures and delights. Our drawing is either one big plate of food or one big stomach or double chin.

 **brilliant** exercise

- Try finding five physical aspects of yourself that you like, and really take note of what people compliment you for.

- For two weeks, try to really enjoy and savour your food. Deny yourself nothing but take longer eating and relishing what you are eating. Notice what the food tastes of and how it feels in your mouth.

- Bring colour to your plate.

- Take a minute before eating to be grateful for your food and the body it feeds.

Mindful eating exercise:

Take a piece of chocolate and eat it as slowly as you can, let it melt on your tongue and stay in your mouth as long as you can. Enjoy this exercise with a friend!

Having fun and getting healthy

Dancing

How often do you go out dancing? My daughter gets withdrawal symptoms if she doesn't get out to salsa; it is much more to her than just a good night out. She says it feeds her soul, she is liberated and energised and she feels the positive effects all week. Dancing is probably one of the best immediate happiness boosters you can do, which might be why every culture in the world dances. When you dance you are connected to others, you can improve your skill and experience flow, and your mind and body are in harmony of purpose. The positive effects on your physical health are obvious but dancing is also a great way to improve your psychological well-being.

A recent study found that hip-hop dancing affects your well-being more than ice-skating or body conditioning.[185]

Music

Remember from earlier chapters that listening to music is one of the top immediate pleasure boosters, and doing any exercise to music both makes it more fun and increases the well-being boost. Dancing to music, marching to music – music is primal, it is spiritual and it is physical as well as mental.

Actively making and playing music, or singing, encourages flow and the emotional connection of playing music with other people ticks almost all well-being factors. It is impossible to play in a band, sing in a choir or play in an orchestra without being aware of and open to other people. Playing an instrument is also a physical activity. The fitness of a drummer is equal to that of an athlete![186] If you sing in a choir or blow a wind instrument you need to have good lungs and breathing is the first healthy activity we started the chapter with. Being actively engaged with making music is a wonderful way to stay healthy. However, we are talking here about being actively engaged, not sitting with a computer alone in your room, so get out and make music with other people if you really want to feel great.

The educational psychologist Susan Hallam lists among the many positive effects of making music:

- Increases positive emotion and energy; music makes you happy and vital!
- Improves your intellect and thinking skills
- Stimulates creativity
- Reduces depression
- Improves general health, improves heart rate, lowers mortality rates
- Improves social skills
- Improves purpose and motivation
- Improves reading and numerate ability in children
- Improves memory.[187]

Physical hobbies and activities

Gardening, riding, canoeing, sailing, skiing, hiking, golf – any activity that is both physical and gets you out in a wonderful environment is food for the soul as well as your muscles. Being outside is good for you, good for your lungs, your heart and your mind. Being actively engaged in pleasurable physical activity that offers challenges and social connection is an easy way to health and well-being.

Being with nature – get outside!

In a recent study it was found that more than just being outside,, being outside surrounded by nature, has a marked effect on energy and well-being. Just 20 minutes a day was enough to boost vitality levels significantly.[188]

Gardening is one of the easiest outdoor activities that will give you great exercise but also offers you the opportunity to care for and create something beautiful. Tending a plant and watching its progress will boost your psychological well-being as well as your physical health. Spending time with many varieties of plants and flowers, their colours, textures and abundance, is an instant de-stressor. Don't make gardening a chore; when the weeds are a little tall or a bed is overgrown, take time to notice the natural beauty of nature. Choose to focus on one thing at a time and remember the power of being mindful; gardening offers many activities that can be almost meditative. If you do have a big job in the garden that is more like a tough chore, then make a ceremony of its completion – find a way to celebrate. Getting your hands into the soil and really getting to grips with the physicality that gardening can offer is brilliant for depression. Monty Don says that he dug his way out of depression.

Be creative and get inventive but get off the sofa. It may be strange to talk about being creative in a chapter on physical well-being, but hobbies that are creative can also be physical. We touched on gardening but getting outside with a sketchbook can get you walking if you love drawing. Taking children on a picnic, walking a dog, getting a group of friends out for the day are all creative ways to get off the sofa.

- How can you combine your strengths and values with an outdoor activity?

Martial arts and physical disciplines

Yoga, tai chi, taekwondo, judo, pilates, gymnastics and poi are becoming increasingly recognised for their psychological as much as physical benefits. The physical benefits are massive, as many Eastern tequniques are designed to improve not just the flexibility of the body but keeping the internal energy lines healthy. When we are heartbroken we tend to hunch in a way that is protective of our heart, and our posture is very connected to our internal and emotional well-being. Research is finding more and more the effect that activities like yoga or judo have on our neurological systems. In Chapter 8 we looked at the benefits of self-regulation and having some self-discipline. Combining self-discipline of both the mind and the body is a really great habit to have in your life and you will notice the effect not only on your fitness but also on the sharpness of your mind and your ability to function better in other areas of your life. Self-regulation is a muscle that improves the more you exercise it.

Sex

Why not pep up your sex life? Sex is one of the best activities in the world for health and happiness.

Sex is physically good for you as it improves your:
- Heart rate
- Respiratory system
- Circulation
- Burns calories
- Supports your immune system
- General health and longevity.[189]

There is a saying that 'A good sex life is part of your life but a bad sex life is the whole of your life.' If you are not happy with your sex life, try using all the chapters in this book to address the issue.

Sex affects not just your physical health but your emotional, psychological and spiritual well-being. Intimacy and connection are improved with touching and being stroked,[190] because being touched gives us masses of feel-good hormones. For women, one good partner is much better than many one-night stands.[191] Everyone is different and you may not be in a monogamous loving relationship, but whatever your situation it is worth remembering that although sex is one of the best positive activities you can engage in, it is not as good for your emotional health if you cause yourself or other people harm.

Take time to make it special, have positive sex:

- Be generous.
- Be kind.
- Be inventive: add variety, try something new sometimes.
- Use your strengths!
- Be grateful.
- Be curious.
- Be real.

How to develop healthy habits

Developing healthy goals involves becoming aware of the need and the intention to find and maintain a programme or strategy to meet that need.

Shifting our energy to make time for activities, even if they offer reward, requires us to change and create new habits. Finding the self-discipline and commitment to a new habit can be hard because often it means we have to choose not to do what we are doing in order to have time for the new thing.

We may love our partners, family and friends and feel great after a good evening with those we love, but often it is easier to collapse in front of the telly rather than fix a date to get out and do something different.

According to Tal Ben-Shahar, who teaches positive psychology at Harvard, creating a new habit takes at least four weeks and he says that you should attempt to start only one habit at a time and that each new habit takes four to six weeks to embed. He also encourages us to follow Loehr and Schwartz,[192] who suggest that making a ritual around new behaviour, doing something at a specific time and in a particular way, makes the motivation to the task or new behaviour much easier when we need some self-discipline. This is even more powerful when the ritual supports our values and has meaning. Ben-Shahar uses cleaning our teeth as an example of a ritual that no longer requires much self-discipline and it is part of our value for ourselves and our hygiene.[193]

 **brilliant** exercise

Create a new habit

- Which *one* healthy habit do you want to put in your life right now?
- Write it down.
- Now write down what creating this habit will give you.
- What values will it reflect?
- What will doing this contribute to who you are and what you stand for?
- Who will you be if you do this?
- What bigger aspect of yourself and your life will it support and value?

Now write down what not doing this new habit will cost you.

What do you need to lose from your life to make time for the new habit?

Using your top strengths in Chapter 4, look again at putting this habit in your life and how you could make a ritual of it and use your strengths. That might be easy if your top strength is being creative, having self-control or being full of zest, but how can gratitude or forgiveness support an exercise programme? What could a 30-minute ritual look like that supported being grateful – a programme that expressed gratitude for all the different working parts of a wonderful body?

brilliant recap

This chapter has got you thinking about the importance of your physical health to your happiness and well-being and that being happy affects your health.

- You have been introduced to how to think more positively about food, drink, your body and exercise.

- Being engaged in activities such as dancing or making music has a significant positive effect on every aspect of our well-being, both physical and mental.

- Getting outside, gardening, playing sport, hiking, bicycling, canoeing, sailing, climbing or even fishing will benefit your mental as well as your physical health and well-being and also give you an opportunity to be in flow.

- Being with nature boosts your vitality and happiness.

- Remember that positive sex is good for you.

I hope that you have chosen to start a new habit that will make you both healthier and happier.

CHAPTER 10

Putting positive psychology to work at work

Every production of genius must be the production of enthusiasim.

Benjamin Disraeli, 1804–81

Positive psychology is having a huge effect in the workplace. This final chapter will tell you what the important factors are that foster well-being, better job satisfaction, better motivation and ultimately more fulfilment in your working life. We will examine all the factors that foster positive emotions and engagement at work. Research shows that organisations using positive psychology in the workplace are finding that not only do they get a happier workforce but also a happier profit margin!

One of the most practical applications of positive psychology is at the workplace. We spend a large part of our lives at work, making it, proportionately, a key component in our general state of well-being. Not being happy at work can not only affect our sense of well-being during office hours, but can significantly affect other areas of our life in a negative way. Additionally, through our personal development, productivity and growth at work, positive psychology can give us actual measurable return, whether that be in:

- Our general satisfaction with life
- Happiness and fulfilment
- Personal success
- Better business relationships
- A promotion or pay rise
- Or just feeling more confident in what you do.

Feeling good at work has been shown to positively affect:

- Teamwork
- Engagement
- Diversity and inclusion
- Attention
- Thinking and performance
- Creativity.

No matter how large or small the workplace is, you can put in some positive psychology and start to get yourself and other people around you more engaged and happy. Put aside the need to be liked, feared, popular, the best team player/leader or make your mark and start by addressing your, and others', need to feel good. At work you have an ideal opportunity to meet many of the needs you require to feel happy and satisfied with your life.

Positive psychology applied to performance and achievement

Happy people are effective people

Research tells us that an environment that fosters positive emotions and engagement within the workforce benefits from higher performance and cognitive ability.[194] When you are engaged you feel excited, happy and energised; you are more focused and connected to what you are doing and as a consequence more creative and better able to problem solve. Becoming more engaged in what you do is key not just to your enjoyment but also to your performance.

🏹 **brilliant** exercise

Can you answer yes to the following questions?

- At work, I have the opportunity to do what I do best every day.
- I know what is expected of me at work.
- I have the materials and equipment I need to do my work right.
- I have the opportunity to learn and grow.
- I have a variety of tasks to complete.
- I have control over my work.
- I use my strengths daily.

Saying yes to these questions would indicate that you have a positive working life.

How to improve engagement at work

1 A strengths-based approach

Working to your strengths is the first route to feeling happier and more engaged; not only will you enjoy using your strengths but the chance of your being in flow also increases. How can you bring a strengths-based focus to your working day?

- List three new ways you are able to use your strengths at work more often.
- List three ways you can encourage other people you work with to recognise and use their strengths.

Refer back to Chapter 4 for a list of strengths or go to www. strengthsfinder.com. Sometimes people have hidden strengths that they have not been given a chance to display. If you work in an environment that allows you to reassign tasks according to the individual strengths of the team, you will be amazed at how much more quickly strategies and goals will fall into place. For every person who tries to escape from spreadsheets and detailed accounting there is someone who leaves skid marks in their enthusiasm to get at those numbers. Some people love standing up and performing while others keep everyone laughing. Recognising others' strengths can be as rewarding as using your own.

- What are your top strengths?
- What are the top strengths of those you work with?
- How can you recognise your co-workers strengths today?
- What strengths in those around you are not being fully utilised and how can you change this?

Using a strengths-based assessment programme is a great way to improve motivation and engagement and you will find details of these at the end of this book

2 Variety

Variety and newness keep us engaged and energised. Remember to use as many strengths as you can, as well as looking for ways to vary what you do. We all fall into ruts and habits; having a great routine is a source of pleasure. However, change and variety also make us feel good.

Randomly reassigning tasks is a great way to mix things up a bit. If you are in a position to do so, actually getting people to change jobs for a day is a very powerful way to build novelty and understanding into a workforce, and it can have remarkably positive effects.[195]

- How can you mix things up a bit, what dynamics can you vary, what can you do differently?

brilliant tip

Get variety into your working life:

- Think of a way to do something routine in a new way.
- Accept a new experience or challenge.
- Try using another strength.
- Be adventurous.
- Say YES.

3 Clear goals

Having clear goals really helps to motivate us. When we know what it is we have to do (and why), we can really get engaged with how we are going to do it. If you are not sure what you are doing or what your goals are, is there any way you can address this?

How to clarify your goals:

- In order to clarify goals, remember to keep them both realistic and achievable in the short term – don't lose the impossible dream, but find something tangible and small that has a clear end.
- Find someone to be accountable to if you are working on your own, and also a date for celebration.
- If you are in a situation where you are being expected to work with unrealistic goals and you are disengaged because you feel overwhelmed or out of control, imagine you have a Harry Potter wand and one flick of the wand would reveal what really matters. Then focus on that.
- Use your strengths to change or improve the situation.
- Remember that feeling good helps you to think clearly, so give yourself a positive boost.

4 Getting flow into your work

Having the opportunity to develop skills and to be challenged is the most rewarding way to be engaged at work. Remember that when we get the chance to improve our skills it is one of the ways we can experience flow. Being challenged improves our abilities, which increases our self-confidence and self-esteem. Are you challenged at work?

How to get flow into your working life:

- Look for opportunities where you can develop skills or learn new skills.
- Find ways to do more of what gets you really excited.
- Accept challenges.
- Create a workspace that is a pleasure to be in.
- Decide to do your job to the highest standard, seek to be excellent and don't cut corners.
- Pay close attention to the task in hand, value each step and process.

How can you create the opportunity for more flow in your workspace for other people?

5 Job clarity

Understanding what is expected of you and those around you matters. Job clarity has been found to positively affect:

- Job satisfaction
- Organisational commitment
- Less anxiety
- Employee well-being.[196]

Much of what modern workers are required to do on the job is dictated by demands that make sense at some higher organisational level but are obscure to the worker.

Mihaly Csikszentmihalyi, 1996

Good leadership knows where it is leading people and to what end; bad leadership gets bogged down in the detail or caught up in the big idea so that it is hard to get properly engaged.

 **exercise**

Take the lift test: try to describe your job to someone in one minute.

If you can't do this, try asking yourself:

● What is the most important aspect of your work to you?

● What is the most important aspect of your work to your company or employer?

If the answer to these questions is not the same, it might be worth examining if this is a problem to you.

6 *Autonomy*

In order to be intrinsically motivated, you need to have a high degree of autonomy.

Having autonomy, having freedom to choose your own actions at work, can be highly motivating and research shows that having individual freedom and being trusted are very effective. A workforce being given responsibility for their own actions are

significantly happier because having more autonomy improves
and supports:

- belongingness
- empowerment
- job satisfaction
- commitment
- citizenship.[197]

 example

The software company Atlassian developed a great idea to give their
workforce autonomy; every three months or so they have 24 hours to work
on whatever they choose, the only proviso being that they have to give
a three-minute presentation the next day on what they were working on.
This process has given birth to some really innovative ideas, and is also an
opportunity for individuals to show more of their skills – and a 'FedEx day'
is fun!

If you are able to give autonomy to others at work, you will really
improve their sense of well-being in their job.

- How much autonomy and intrinsic motivation do you have
  at work?
- Are you able to choose how you go about your work?
- Do you have freedom to work to your strengths?
- Do you have goals that are your own and are exciting to
  you?

brilliant example

A brilliant example of the power of intrinsic motivation is the success of Wikipedia over Microsoft's Encarta dictionary. Although Microsoft had all the right paid incentives in place to deliver Encarta, the most popular online dictionary today is Wikipedia. Written by unpaid contributors, the motivation of the Wikipedia writers is purely intrinsic as they write the entries and keep things up to date just because they are passionate about the subject matter.

7 Mindset

A growth mindset at work is especially important if you hold any kind of leadership role. Having a growth mindset means being open to change, and, more importantly, open to growth, in yourself as much as in others. Do you have a mindset that sees failure as an opportunity to learn? In his book, *From Good to Great*, Jim Collins[198] found that one of the common attributes of leaders who created great companies was their ability to address failure, even their own, and they were always questioning how they could improve and learn.

People with open mindsets are more likely to surround themselves with bright challenging people and are also not afraid to employ people who are more able than they are.

The psychologist Carol Dweck believes that having a growth mindset is essential to good leadership because leaders see talent as the start of the potential development of their employees.[199]

brilliant example

Robert Wood and Albert Bandura found that business students with a growth mindset outperformed students with fixed mindsets. The students

▶ in the first group were given a fixed mindset by being told that their natural ability was to be measured by the tasks they were set, whereas the students given a growth mindset were told that in order to perform the tasks they would learn as they went along. Not only did the 'learners' out-perform those relying on their inherent ability but at the end of the study they were more confident.[200]

Positive psychology applied to business relationships

Everything we do requires that we are able to communicate and work with other people. Whatever the nature of your work, it can be made better or worse by other people. Everything that we covered in Chapter 5 about emotional intelligence is brilliant in the workplace but there is much more to how other people can affect how well we flourish at work.

Being happy makes us more effective and creative. When we are happy we like being where we are and doing what we are doing. We have looked at activities that help us to become more engaged and perform better; now we will look at what makes us feel recognised and connected at work. Our relationships with other people are a huge reason why we enjoy work.

brilliant insight

The positive emotions which are key to engagement and well-being in the workplace are: joy, interest and love.

Can you answer yes to the following statements?

● In the last seven days, I have received recognition and praise for doing good work.

- My supervisor or someone at work seems to care about me personally.
- There is someone at work who encourages my development.
- At work my opinions count.
- I have a best friend at work.
- In the last six months, someone at work talked to me about my progress.[201]

Being supported, cared about and feeling that you are also contributing and giving something tangible to the organisation appear to be a universal quality of employee engagement across all organisations and businesses. Organisations that foster these emotions in their workforce also benefit from higher performance and cognitive ability. Happiness directly affects job satisfaction and performance and this is most marked by altruistic behaviour and generosity to other people.[202]

How to improve communication and relatedness at work

1 Recognition

Having someone recognise what we have achieved and celebrating with us might seem too obvious to mention; everyone likes to be acknowledged but it is also great to acknowledge other people. Whatever your role or position at work, it is always possible to recognise other people if only to thank them. A genuine thank you is very simple and makes a huge difference. A short e-mail or text is quite acceptable, but it is now such a universal way to communicate that it is easy to forget the power of a handwritten note or card.

brilliant tip

Making time to celebrate successes or even just a good week can happen over lunch or after work. I met a company director who thanked his sales managers by sending flowers to their partners at their place of work to acknowledge the partners' support, understanding that they probably contributed to the sales managers' success.

- Think about how you can bring thanks and recognition into your working life.
- Be inventive, remember reciprocity, be the first to be generous with your thanks.
- Keep it genuine and real.

2 Friendship

Top of the list for well-being and happiness is having good friends. We spend so much of our life at work that it is no surprise that friendship at work is an important feel-good factor. It is not always possible to have friends at work, especially if you work alone or from home. Friends give you confidence and support, they provide you with someone to confide in and guide you through difficult times and in the workplace thay can often help practically with information and knowledge.

- Value working colleagues.
- Set aside time for lunch with a friend or colleague.
- Offer support when you are able and it is appropriate; a team effort is good in any circumstances.
- Work on your collaboration skills.
- Seek collaboration with someone you enjoy spending time with.

3 Positive structure and support

Friends are great but the support from above is the most effective at reducing stress at work.

Having a supervisor who is considerate, encouraging and helpful has a big effect on employee job satisfaction and, conversely, problems with supervisors are one of the most common causes of unhappiness and conflict.

Factors that assist positive structure and support are:

- Back-reporting
- Feedback
- Job clarity.

 **insight**

The research shows that job satisfaction and employee well-being are profoundly affected by employees knowing what they are doing and that they can manage it.[203]

---

4 Positive teamwork

Being part of a good team makes us happy. How can you create a feeling of team spirit within your organisation? Find time as a team to focus on what has worked in the past and reinvent the future using this collective knowledge. Think of the organisation in which you work and tailor your team spirit accordingly. Create an ethos that is inclusive. Research shows that integrating the ethos of the company in a way that involves the individual creates a better team spirit.

5 Build trust

Use some of the skills from the last chapter.

- How well do you really listen?
- How much do you allow yourself to be quiet and present to those around you?

- What are people saying between the lines?
- How can your strengths support you to hold the space as much as lead the way?

 exercise

Try back-reporting, which means repeating back in your own words the importance and meaning at the heart of what someone is telling you. You can start by saying something like 'What I think you wanted me to understand was ...' Obviously, don't do this inappropriately!

Any conversation or communication that requires your attention or action can be powerfully supported in this way. If it is not appropriate to repeat back what someone has just told you, try repeating what they have said to yourself in such a way that it is as if you are listening to them for a second time.

6 Generosity

Remember what Jonathan Haidt tells us about the power of 'tit for tat'. This is as relevant in the workplace as anywhere. We are much happier to give work and support to someone who has given the same to us. There are many business networking models based on this principle, that those to whom we give business are more likely to refer business back to us. Giving away free gifts is based on the same principle. However, don't be cynical or manipulative; genuine generosity is good for **your** well-being and that applies as much in the workplace as anywhere.

7 Look at what works

As we saw in Chapter 4, focusing on what works is much more energising than worrying over what doesn't. David Cooperrider has designed a great way to facilitate organisations to develop successful past outcomes and use what has worked in new and innovative ways to great effect. The process is called Appreciative Inquiry and can involve any number of people across an organisation.[204]

↗ brilliant exercise

Take time to remember and share successful events from your life or from the company's life with someone else. Together ask each other what made these events work, what the factors were, who was with you, what motivated you, what was successful, what worked. The events can be from any part of your experience but as you share and question each other, aspects of what worked and the strengths utilised will emerge. You can then start to imagine new ways to integrate what worked from the past into current issues and reimagine future events and goals.

---

8 *The role of optimism and pessimism*

Optimists believe that they have much more control over events and situations than they actually do; this is a great coping mechanism in stressful situations. Remember that optimistic thinking is better at problem solving and can reframe situations to see them in a better light. In the workplace, problem solving and facing up to situations are an asset; however, pessimists are more realistic in bad situations, and although they can lack perseverance and may avoid facing up to things, they are often better at the detail. Sometimes we need a pessimistic outlook.

Optimism and pessimism in the workplace

	Attributes	Negatives
Optimists	Problem solve, reframe, persevere, face up to situations, emotionally well equipped to handle stress	Unrealistic in bad situations, low attention to detail

▷

	Attributes	Negatives
Pessimist	More realistic about negative events/situations, better at detailed work such as accountancy	Tendency to avoid bad situations

Positive psychology and meaningful work

The following statements are all important factors in well-being and happiness at work:

- The mission/purpose of my company makes me feel my job is important.

- My associates (fellow employees) are committed to doing quality work.

- I have opportunity for personal growth.[205]

When your talents and values match your job you are much happier; meaningful work is work that holds meaning for you. In an environment that matches your individual values you are more likely to find opportunities to attain goals that matter.[206]

Positive psychology is also finding that effective organisations shift their emphasis from getting more out of people to investing more in them.

One of the best ways to increase energy in the workplace is to increase a sense of purpose and meaning. There are three ways in which people describe their work:

- As a job – you go to work because you have to and it pays the bills.

- As a career – there is a structure and plan to your working life; you may not necessarily be in the job of your dreams but you are working towards it.

- As a calling – your work is a vocation. It has intrinsic meaning and purpose, and you feel a sense of connectedness to more than your own needs. Your personal mission and values match the organisation's and you love what you do.

brilliant insight

Ken Robinson talks about how we are groomed from a very early age to set our sights high in terms of the work we do. He uses the example of a very bright pupil who talks of wanting to be a fireman only to be told that he should think of doing something more valuable with his life. Some years later he pulls the teacher and his wife from a car wreck and asks if saving their lives is a valuable enough way to spend his time. What could be more valuable than to spend your life both happily and meaningfully?[207]

We are most happy and fulfilled in the third category, 'as a calling', but many of us are not lucky enough to know what it is we want to do and to spend our lives doing it. However, all jobs can be a calling if you choose to show up and use your strengths, develop an attitude of service or see it as part of something worthwhile. The only difference between a job and a calling is the attitude and skills you bring into it.

Ways to make your job a calling:

- Look to the needs of others; be generous, show compassion and empathy.
- Become self-aware; know what you believe in, value, and what motivates you and be prepared to stand up for what you believe in.
- Have vision and principles and do your job according to these principles.
- Learn and grow. Use your mistakes and setbacks as experience that informs and builds what you do. Develop a growth mindset.

- Celebrate the difference in others.
- Believe in yourself and develop courage in that belief.
- Look to understand and get to the bottom of things, try to see the bigger picture.
- Be present and open to the moment.
- Find what you want to serve; work in a way that is meaningful to you.

Here are some examples of making work more meaningful within a wider life context. Any job can be injected with more purpose and direction just by where you put your focus and attention:

- The money feeds my children and my family: this is what matters most to me; I feel productive and honest.
- It offers the opportunity and challenge to engage with and make each customer/client feel better in some way. I cannot live without excellence and creativity.
- Some of the money earned is going towards dancing lessons – the job is helping me move towards where I really want to be. In the meantime I try to get out dancing and performing as much as I can and I have the opportunity to perform at work.
- It is a step towards management/promotion. I love both the business edge and service of the business and this orderly environment suits me. My purpose is to bring order in a supportive way to those I work for and with.
- The business has a green policy and I can contribute to making my colleagues more aware of green issues. Being connected to a bigger picture matters to me. What I do is an important part of something bigger.
- I work with people who make me laugh every day. I have friendship and recognition.
- Everything I do today will be: fun, done well, done for others, done with curiosity, done with enthusiasm, done with attention, etc.

Transformational leadership

Leadership in any organisation shapes and makes it, leadership is both the shipbuilder and the helmsman but as helmsman it is hands on and involved. The qualities of the transformational leader include:

- Clear leadership that can communicate the value and meaning of the vision of the organisation and the direction in which it is headed.
- People working under this form of leadership are rewarded intrinsically. They are encouraged to think for themselves, are recognised for their potential and given opportunities for self-development and growth.
- Transformational leadership is empathetic and seeks to foster leadership; it is team minded.[208]

These aspects of leadership build trust, recognition, commitment and pride in the organisation, key factors in feeling happy and satisfied at work.

 Lead from the back, and let others believe they are in front.

Nelson Mandela

Happiness at work

Happiness at work is a serious business and there are many important factors that are all interconnected. The value of positive emotion in the workplace is huge for the effects on cognitive, problem-solving and creative abilities. Positive psychologists believe that an environment that offers autonomy, the chance to do well, in a team-based context under transformational leadership offers the best opportunity to be happy and flourish.[209] Feeling that what we do and that who we are matter in a safe environment gives people the energy that fuels creativity and potential. Everything that feeds all these needs ultimately fuels happiness, a healthy engagement at work and the opportunity to develop and grow.

Measuring and looking at the factors that contribute to how good we feel at work is an increasingly complex issue that is necessarily not linear. In the past 20 years business has moved far beyond accepting that the only guides to predicting success are IQ or psychometric testing and now many more factors such as happiness and emotional intelligence are recognised for their importance. It is becoming more and more evident that flourishing businesses, like flourishing people, are doing *many* things right and that happiness, although a vital factor, is not the whole story. Real flourishing at work happens under resilient and wise leadership that is open to all positive and meaningful practices. Fulfilment at work happens when we feel we matter and are recognised for doing something we love to do, but keeping a whole workforce flourishing and motivated requires passion and resilience.

 **brilliant** recap

This chapter has shown you how positive psychology is an asset in the workplace. There is no question that being who we are and attending to all that we are is a recurring theme. Positive psychology is proving again and again that success and material gain are not the most important part of a happy, fulfilled and flourishing life.

- We have looked at how people need to feel fulfilled by what they do.

- Many people speak of finding part of that fulfilment in the relationships that they have at work as much as in the work itself.

- At work, whatever you do, there is probably the greatest opportunity to grow and develop, to develop your emotional intelligence, empathy and self-knowledge.

- At work you can push yourself to face challenges and reach your potential with the support of others and to give other people the chance to find their own talents and strengths.

- A happy workplace offers trust, recognition and commitment that are reflected both in leadership and in individuals.

I hope that from this chapter you take away some hope and excitement about bringing more happiness and meaning to your working life and that each day becomes an adventure and an opportunity to create what you were born to do.

What did you think of this book?

We're really keen to hear from you about this book, so that we can make our publishing even better.

Please log on to the following website and leave us your feedback.

It will only take a few minutes and your thoughts are invaluable to us.

www.pearsoned.co.uk/bookfeedback

Afterword

This book has only scratched the surface of positive psychology but I hope it has given you insight into what contributes most to your happiness and well-being.

For me there are three key subjects to keep in mind with everything in this book. The first is choice; we began with choice, so it is fitting that we should end there. The second is complexity and the final subject is creativity.

Choice

We **can** choose, we can choose how we think, feel and act. And how we choose affects all our experiences.

After reading this book you may choose to:

- Be more grateful
- Be more generous and kind
- Think more optimistically
- Have more fun
- Go for that goal and choose to commit to it
- Choose how you perceive events, other people and the world around you
- Practise mindfulness
- See the beauty and abundance around you

- Live to your values
- Have a healthier time perspective
- Accept yourself and celebrate your and other people's strengths
- Look for meaning and purpose in your life
- Exercise more and eat better.

In fact, I hope that you will decide to **choose more** and build your autonomy, because you and you alone are the creator of your life. Nelson Mandela has revealed the strength he drew from this knowledge: that when you have no other control in your life you can still choose to control your thoughts. He is the shining example in our time of the power of this ability.

Complexity

I hope that you have noticed that there isn't just one contributing key to a happier, more fulfilled life. Nothing is simple and yet everything is simple, because changing just one small aspect in your life affects something else, which in turn has an effect.

The scientist Stephen Wolfran shows very neatly how complexity can arise from the very simple when randomness is one of the factors fed into the most basic computer program. This is not what is interesting; his main point is that it is not always possible to retrieve the simple beginning from the complex or to predict the outcome when randomness is a feature. In a very simple example he creates beautiful and complex patterns from running very basic programs.[210]

In some ways it could be said that positive psychology is attempting to find the code, the initial program that produces the most beautiful lives. Philosophers and mystics have attempted similar journeys and come to very similar conclusions. There is no surprise at how much research findings are mirroring some of the teachings of ancient mystics and philosophers. However, it should be remembered that all ancient writings on the practices and behaviours of those who have embodied what has been recognised as the height of human flourishing were written by followers in their name. Buddha, Jesus and Socrates **wrote nothing**. Their 'teaching' was given in practice and through stories and principles that call for reflective action in relationship to the self and others; the best understanding of these teachings is only really revealed in practice.

Scientists are always seeking to reduce things to the smallest element and then invest all understanding and explanation of the complex from the small and the individual, yet at the very smallest level it appears nothing can be separated from the inquiry or scientific intent. Human life is not isolated, even within itself. Each thought, word and deed is in communion with otherness: our environment or someone else or our own desires and needs, ambitions or fears, with the added extra of the random feedback loop that each thought generates as it ricochets out and back like an echosounder.

When people are happier they are kinder, more generous, more grateful, and healthier. When people open themselves up to growth and compassion, empathy and connectedness, more lives flourish than just that of the individual. Just as micro-financing is recognised as a powerful force for change in building the economic strength of communities from within, so positive psychology is showing us how much the smallest attention to how we look at the world and those around us can affect not just our own well-being but everything around us. Positive psychology is seeking to extend this message in a way that opens up opportunities for individuals to flourish from childhood to old age. Every time you choose to learn, grow and develop personally you change more than your own abilities and well-being. The simplest change in thinking or behaviour can have a far-reaching effect.

We are complicated, and we live in a world that is complex beyond even science's ability to grasp fully, but the complex arises from the very small and the very simple. The butterfly effect can be seen in much of the research in positive psychology. Remember Barbara Fredrickson telling us that there is an important ratio of positive effect that has a tipping point, 3:1 positive to negative. This is similar to the effects found in chaos theory. Just as the butterfly flapping its wings can cause a hurricane, each small change you make in your life matters. The old proverb, 'For want of a nail the horse was lost, for want of a horse the rider was lost, for want of a rider the battle was lost, for want of a battle the kingdom was lost, and all for the want of a horseshoe nail',[211] sums it up nicely.

A small caution

A happy fulfilled life as the subject for study and understanding is important.[212] However, looking for **the** key to happiness and well-being can inspire prescriptive ideals. History is littered with the casualties of putting into practice ideas that claim to lead to a good and happy life. It is with this caution in mind that this book should be read. Positive psychology is at the forefront of a scientific approach to understanding what makes us flourish and could claim to 'know' the answers, but proving one thing and acting on that proof can have unforeseen consequences elsewhere. For example, 25 years ago psychological research discovered the correlation between depression and low self-esteem. Boosting self-esteem became the holy grail of psychologists. However, after more study into the concept, high self-esteem has been found to be great for the individual while not good for others. People with high self-esteem are more likely to be aggressive and bully others, are more likely to cheat and to be self-serving generally at others' expense. High self-esteem can have negative consequences.[213] Like our modern obsession with food, we may find that eating blueberries reduces the risk of cancer and heart disease but we also know that a diet of only blueberries would be poisonous. Time and again the research reveals the power of variety. Your strengths can be your weakness if they are overused or used too narrowly, and your talents and skills grow better when challenged in a new way.

The research to date, the subject and business of positive psychology, should be used to inform and guide rather than dictate. The subjective context in which happiness and well-being are experienced is a complicated and perpetual interplay of how and why we think and how and why we feel, which is both genetic and learned. The happy news is that we **can** affect the quality of our life and how we feel.

Creativity

Creativity is the unmentioned subject of this book but is the expression of all aspects of a flourishing life. Everything we do is creative or has the potential to create. Every time we smile at someone we create a moment. Being creative is who we are in action, any action, in our work, with our family and friends, and most especially in the effect we have on our environment. Shelling peas can be a creative process and we are all performance artists like Gilbert and George; our life IS our creation and when we flourish we create better.

In comfort and luxury some people can create hell, and in the worst degradation and shortage there are people who can create heaven. It is truly your choice: *'Believe that life is worth living, and your belief will create the fact'* (William James, 1842–1910).

Mindmap

I have included a mindmap, which at first glance looks a little alarming (Figure A.1). It is not definitive but the arrows represent proven causal links; if **all** the integrated effects of our actions and thoughts were able to be put on one page in this way it would be a spider's web. The map should show you that all things affect all things. I wish I had been able to represent it in 3D, because as you work on areas of your life the circle of effect is the same, but you can spiral upwards. As you grow and develop, one aspect in your life will suddenly change and suddenly everything is affected.

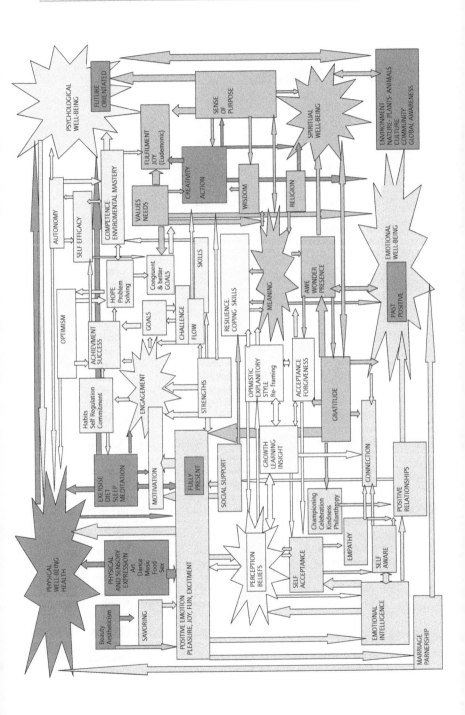

List of values

1 Abundance	37 Benevolence	73 Consistency
2 Acceptance	38 Bliss	74 Contentment
3 Accessibility	39 Boldness	75 Continuity
4 Accomplishment	40 Bravery	76 Contribution
5 Accuracy	41 Brilliance	77 Control
6 Achievement	42 Buoyancy	78 Conviction
7 Acknowledgement	43 Calmness	79 Conviviality
8 Activeness	44 Camaraderie	80 Coolness
9 Adaptability	45 Candour	81 Cooperation
10 Adoration	46 Capability	82 Cordiality
11 Adroitness	47 Care	83 Correctness
12 Adventure	48 Carefulness	84 Courage
13 Affection	49 Cautious	85 Courtesy
14 Affluence	50 Celebrity	86 Craftiness
15 Aggressiveness	51 Certainty	87 Creativity
16 Agility	52 Challenge	88 Credibility
17 Alertness	53 Charity	89 Cunning
18 Altruism	54 Charm	90 Curiosity
19 Ambition	55 Chastity	91 Daring
20 Amusement	56 Cheerfulness	92 Decisiveness
21 Anticipation	57 Clarity	93 Decorum
22 Appreciation	58 Cleanliness	94 Deference
23 Approachability	59 Clear-mindedness	95 Delight
24 Articulacy	60 Cleverness	96 Dependability
25 Assertiveness	61 Closeness	97 Depth
26 Assurance	62 Comfort	98 Desire
27 Attentiveness	63 Commitment	99 Determination
28 Attractiveness	64 Compassion	100 Devotion
29 Audacity	65 Completion	101 Devoutness
30 Availability	66 Composure	102 Dexterity
31 Awareness	67 Concentration	103 Dignity
32 Awe	68 Confidence	104 Diligence
33 Balance	69 Conformity	105 Direction
34 Beauty	70 Congruency	106 Directness
35 Being the best	71 Connection	107 Discipline
36 Belonging	72 Consciousness	108 Discovery

109 Discretion
110 Diversity
111 Dominance
112 Dreaming
113 Drive
114 Duty
115 Dynamism
116 Eagerness
117 Economy
118 Ecstasy
119 Education
120 Effectiveness
121 Efficiency
122 Elation
123 Elegance
124 Empathy
125 Encouragement
126 Endurance
127 Energy
128 Enjoyment
129 Entertainment
130 Enthusiasm
131 Excellence
132 Excitement
133 Exhilaration
134 Expectancy
135 Expediency
136 Experience
137 Expertise
138 Exploration
139 Expressiveness
140 Extravagance
141 Extroversion
142 Exuberance
143 Fairness
144 Faith
145 Fame
146 Family
147 Fascination
148 Fashion
149 Fearlessness
150 Ferocity
151 Fidelity
152 Fierceness
153 Financial
    independence
154 Firmness
155 Fitness

156 Flexibility
157 Flow
158 Fluency
159 Focus
160 Fortitude
161 Frankness
162 Freedom
163 Friendliness
164 Frugality
165 Fun
166 Gallantry
167 Generosity
168 Gentility
169 Giving
170 Grace
171 Gratitude
172 Growth
173 Guidance
174 Happiness
175 Harmony
176 Health
177 Heart
178 Helpfulness
179 Heroism
180 Holiness
181 Honesty
182 Honour
183 Hopefulness
184 Hospitality
185 Humility
186 Humour
187 Hygiene
188 Imagination
189 Impact
190 Impartiality
191 Independence
192 Industry
193 Ingenuity
194 Inquisitiveness
195 Insightfulness
196 Inspiration
197 Integrity
198 Intelligence
199 Intensity
200 Intimacy
201 Intrepidness
202 Introversion
203 Intuition

204 Intuitiveness
205 Inventiveness
206 Investing
207 Joy
208 Judiciousness
209 Justice
210 Keenness
211 Kindness
212 Knowledge
213 Leadership
214 Learning
215 Liberation
216 Liberty
217 Liveliness
218 Logic
219 Longevity
220 Love
221 Loyalty
222 Making a difference
223 Mastery
224 Maturity
225 Meekness
226 Mellowness
227 Meticulousness
228 Mindfulness
229 Modesty
230 Motivation
231 Mysteriousness
232 Neatness
233 Nerve
234 Obedience
235 Open-mindedness
236 Openness
237 Optimism
238 Order
239 Organisation
240 Originality
241 Outlandishness
242 Outrageousness
243 Passion
244 Peace
245 Perceptiveness
246 Perfection
247 Perseverance
248 Persistence
249 Persuasiveness
250 Philanthropy
251 Piety

252 Playfulness
253 Pleasantness
254 Pleasure
255 Poise
256 Polish
257 Popularity
258 Potency
259 Power
260 Practicality
261 Pragmatism
262 Precision
263 Preparedness
264 Presence
265 Privacy
266 Proactivity
267 Professionalism
268 Prosperity
269 Prudence
270 Punctuality
271 Purity
272 Realism
273 Reason
274 Reasonableness
275 Recognition
276 Recreation
277 Refinement
278 Reflection
279 Relaxation
280 Reliability
281 Religiousness
282 Resilience
283 Resolution
284 Resolve
285 Resourcefulness
286 Respect
287 Rest
288 Restraint
289 Reverence
290 Richness
291 Rigour

292 Romance
293 Sacredness
294 Sacrifice
295 Sagacity
296 Saintliness
297 Sanguinity
298 Satisfaction
299 Security
300 Self-control
301 Selflessness
302 Self-reliance
303 Sensitivity
304 Sensuality
305 Serenity
306 Service
307 Sexuality
308 Sharing
309 Shrewdness
310 Significance
311 Silence
312 Silliness
313 Simplicity
314 Sincerity
315 Skilfulness
316 Solidarity
317 Solitude
318 Speed
319 Spirit
320 Spirituality
321 Spontaneity
322 Stability
323 Stillness
324 Strength
325 Structure
326 Success
327 Support
328 Supremacy
329 Surprise
330 Sympathy
331 Synergy

332 Teamwork
333 Temperance
334 Thankfulness
335 Thoroughness
336 Thoughtfulness
337 Thrift
338 Tidiness
339 Timeliness
340 Traditionalism
341 Tranquillity
342 Transcendence
343 Trust
344 Trustworthiness
345 Truth
346 Understanding
347 Unflappability
348 Uniqueness
349 Unity
350 Usefulness
351 Utility
352 Valour
353 Variety
354 Victory
355 Vigour
356 Virtue
357 Vision
358 Vitality
359 Vivacity
360 Warmth
361 Wariness
362 Wealth
363 Wilfulness
364 Willingness
365 Winning
366 Wisdom
367 Wittiness
368 Wonder
369 Youthfulness

Useful bibliography

General

Argyle, M. (2001). *The Psychology of Happiness*. East Sussex: Routledge.

Boniwell, I. (2006). *Positive Psychology in a Nutshell*. London: PWBC.

Carr, A. (2004). *Positive Psychology*. East Sussex: Routledge.

Csikszentmihalyi, M. and Csikszentmihalyi, I.S. (eds) (2006). *A Life Worth Living: Contributions to positive psychology*. Oxford: Oxford University Press.

Diener, E., Emmons, R., Larson, J. and Griffin, S. (1985). The Satisfaction with Life Scale. *Journal of Personality Assessment*, 49(1), 71–5.

Diener, E., Suh, E.M., Lucas, R.E. and Smith, H.L. (1999). Subjective well-being: Three decades of progress. *Psychological Bulletin*, 125(2), 276–302.

Fredrickson, B.L. (2009). *Positivity: Groundbreaking research reveals how to embrace the hidden strength of positive emotions, overcome negativity, and thrive*. New York: Crown.

Linley, A. and Joseph, S. (eds) (2004). *Positive Psychology in Practice*. Hoboken, NJ: John Wiley and Sons.

Myers, D.G. (1992). *The Pursuit of Happiness*. New York: Avon Books.

Peterson, C. (2006). *A Primer in Positive Psychology*. Oxford: Oxford University Press.

Seligman, M.E.P. (2003). *Authentic Happiness*. London: Nicholas Brealey.

Seligman, M.E.P. and Csikszentmihalyi, M. (2000). Positive psychology: An introduction. *American Psychologist*, 55, 5–14. Download from: www.ppc.sas.upenn.edu/ppintroarticle.pdf.

Happiness

Ben-Shahar, T. (2008). *Happier: Can you learn to be happy?* Maidenhead UK: McGraw-Hill.

Ben-Shahar, T. (2010). *Even Happier: A gratitude journal for daily joy and lasting fulfilment*. New York: McGraw-Hill.

Diener, E. and Seligman, M. (2002). Very happy people. *Psychological Science*, 13(1), 81–4.

Fredrickson, B. (2003). The value of positive emotions. *American Scientist*, 91, 330–5.

Fredrickson, B. and Marcial, F.L. (2005). Positive affect and the complex dynamics of human flourishing. *American Psychologist*, 60, 678–86.

Fredrickson, B.L. (2009). *Positivity: Groundbreaking research reveals how to embrace the hidden strength of positive emotions, overcome negativity, and thrive*. New York: Crown.

H.H. Dalai Lama and Cutler, H. (1999). *The Art of Happiness: A handbook for living*. London: Hodder and Stoughton.

Haidt, J. (2006). *The Happiness Hypothesis: Finding modern truth in ancient wisdom*. New York: Basic Books.

Lyubomirski, S. (2007). *The How of Happiness: A practical guide to getting the life you want*. London: Sphere.

Nettle, D. (2005). *Happiness: The science behind your smile.* Oxford: Oxford University Press.

Ricard, M. (2007). *Happiness: A guide to developing life's most important skill.* London: Atlantic Books.

Resilience

Briers, S. (2009). *Brilliant: Cognitive behavioural therapy.* Harlow: Pearson Education.

James, Oliver (2007). *Affluenza.* London: Vermilion.

Reivich, K. and Shatté, A. (2003). *The Resilience Factor.* New York: Broadway Books.

Seligman, M. (2006). *Learned Optimism: How to change your mind and your life.* New York: First Vintage Books.

Emotional intelligence

Goleman, D. (2004). *Emotional Intelligence.* London: Bloomsbury.

Flow

Csikszentmihalyi, M. (1990). *Flow: The psychology of optimal experience.* New York: Harper and Row.

Csikszentmihalyi, M. (1997). *Finding flow: The psychology of engagement with everyday life.* New York: Basic Books.

Choice

Schwartz, B. (2004). *The Paradox of Choice.* New York: Harper Perennial.

Gratitude

Emmons, R.A. and McCullough, M.E. (2003). Counting blessings versus burdens: An experimental investigation of gratitude and subjective well-being in daily life. *Journal of Personality and Social Psychology*, 84(2), 377–89.

Mindset

Dweck, C. (2008). *Mindset: The new psychology of success – how we can learn to fulfil our potential*. New York: Ballantine Books.

Strengths

Linley, P.A. and Harrington, S. (2006). *Playing to your strengths. The Psychologist*, 19, 86–9.

Park, N., Peterson, C., and Seligman, M.E.P. (2006). Strengths in 54 nations and the 50 US states. *Journal of Positive Psychology*, 1, 118–29.

Peterson, C. (2006). The Values in Action (VIA) classification of strengths: The un-DSM and the real DSM. In M. Csikszentmihalyi and I.S. Csikszentmihalyi (eds), *A Life Worth Living: Contributions to positive psychology*. New York: Oxford University Press, pp. 29–48.

Web links

www.authentichappiness.sas.upenn.edu
www.centreforconfidence.co.uk
www.ccapeu.com
www.positivepsychology.org.uk
www.breathe-london.com/positive-psychology
www.positivepsychologynews.com
www.mkzc.org/beginzen.html
www.thetimeparadox.com/surveys/ztpi
www.compassionlab.org/teaching.htm
www.gallup.com

References

1. D. Kahneman, A. Krueger, D. Schkade, N. Schwarz and A. Stone (June 2006). Would you be happier if you were richer? *Science*, 312(5782), 1908–10; E. Diener, E.M. Suh, R.E. Lucas and H.L. Smith (1999). *Psychological Bulletin*, 125(2), 288; A. Carr (2004). *Positive Psychology: The science of human happiness*, p. 27, adapted from David G. Myers (2000). The funds, friends and faith of happy people. *American Psychologist*, 55, 56–67.

2. R.A. Emmons and M.E. McCullough (2003). Counting blessings versus burdens: An experimental investigation of gratitude and subjective well-being in daily life. *Journal of Personality and Social Psychology*, 84(2), 377–89.

3. E.W. Dunn, L.B. Aknin, and M.I. Norton (2008). Spending money on others promotes happiness. *Science*, 319, 1687–8.

4. J. Henry (2006). Strategies for achieving well-being. In M. Csikszentmihalyi and I.S. Csikszentmihalyi (eds), *A Life Worth Living*. Oxford: Oxford University Press, pp. 120–38.

5. Ibid., p. 135.

6. Alan Carr (2004). *Positive Psychology: The science of human happiness and human strengths*. London: Routledge, p. 7; David G. Myers (2000). The funds, friends and faith of happy people. *American Psychologist*, 55, 56–67.

7. Sonja Lyubomirsky (2007). *The How of Happiness: A practical guide to getting what you want*. London: Sphere.

8. B. Schwartz, A. Ward, J. Monterosso, S. Lyubomirsky, K. White and D. Lehman (2002). Maximizing versus satisfying; Happiness is a matter of choice. *Journal of Personality and Social Psychology*, 83, 1178–97.

[9] P. Brickman, D. Coates and R. Janoff-Bulman (1978). Lottery winners and accident victims: Is happiness relative? *Journal of Personality and Social Psychology*, 36, 917–27.

[10] Lyubomirsky, ibid., pp. 20–68.

[11] Lyubomirsky, ibid., p. 23.

[12] Kahlil Gibran (1980). *The Prophet*. London: William Heinemann, p. 36.

[13] Mark E. Koltko-Rivera (2006). Rediscovering the later version of Maslow's hierarchy of needs: Self-transcendence and opportunities for theory, research, and unification. *Review of General Psychology*, 10(4), 302–17.

[14] Carol Ryff (1989). Happiness is everything, or is it? Explorations on the meaning of psychological well being. *Journal of Personality and Social Psychology*, 6, 1069–81.

[15] Alois Stutzer and Bruno S. Frey (2008). Stress that doesn't pay: The commuting paradox. *Scandinavian Journal of Economics*, 110(2), 339–66.

[16] E. Langer and J. Rodin (1976). The effects of enhanced personal responsibility for the aged: A field experiment in and institutional setting. *Journal of Personality and Social Psychology*, 34, 191–8.

[17] E. Deci (1971). Effects of externally mediated rewards on intrinsic motivation. *Journal of Personality and Social Psychology*, 18, 105–15.

[18] K.O. McGraw and J. Fiala (1982). Undermining the Zeigarnik effect: Another hidden cost of reward. *Journal of Personality*, 50(1), 58–66.

[19] Carol Dweck (2006). *Mindset: The new psychology of success*. New York: Ballantine Books.

[20] Ibid., p. 12.

[21] Ibid., p. 13.

[22] C. Ryff, ibid., p. 13.

[23] E. Diener and M. Seligman (2002). Very happy people. *Psychological Science*, 13(1), 84.

[24] Alan Carr, ibid., pp. 72–81.

[25] M. Argyle (2001). *The Psychology of Happiness*. London: Routledge, p. 85.

[26] Wood 1989.

[27] Argyle, ibid., p. 85.

28. P.R. Kunz and M. Woolcott (1976). Season's greetings: From my status to yours. *Social Science Research*, 5, 269–78.

29. W. Mischel, Y. Shoda and M.L. Rodriguez (1989). Delay of gratification in children. *Science*, 244, 933–8.

30. Ilona Boniwell (2005). Beyond time management: How the latest research on time perspective and perceived time use can assist clients with time related concern. *International Journal of Evidence Based Coaching and Mentoring*, 3(2), 61–4.

31. Ilona Boniwell, ibid., p. 60.

32. Sheena S. Lyengar and Mark R. Lepper (2000). When choice is demotivating: Can one desire too much of a good thing? *Journal of Personality and Social Psychology*, 79(6), 995–1006.

33. See Barry Schwartz talking at www.Tedtalks.com.

34. See Barry Schwartz and Andrew Ward (2004). Doing better but feeling worse: The paradox of choice. In P.A. Linley and S. Joseph (eds), *Positive Psychology in Practice*. Hoboken, NJ: John Wiley and Sons, pp. 86–104.

35. You can check out your maximiser score at www.swarthmore.edu/SocSci/bschwar1/Sci.Amer.pdf.

36. S. Lyubormirsky and L. Ross (1997). Hedonic consequences of social comparison: A contrast of happy and unhappy people. *Journal of Personality and Social Psychology*, 73, 137–5.

37. Schwartz and Ward (2004), ibid., p. 101.

38. Argyle (1987), ibid., p. 31.

39. B. Fredrickson (2003). The value of positive emotions. *American Scientist*, 91, 330–5.

40. Ibid., p. 333.

41. B. Fredrickson (2005). Positive emotions. In C.R. Snyder and S.J. Lopez (eds), *Handbook of Positive Psychology*. Oxford: Oxford University Press, pp. 120–33; S. Lyubomirsky, L.A. King and E. Diener (2005). The benefits of frequent positive affect: Does happiness lead to success? *Psychological Bulletin*, 131(6), 803–55.

42. Ibid., p. 804.

43. B.L. Fredrickson (2001). The role of positive emotions in positive psychology: The broaden-and-build theory of positive emotions. *American Psychologist*, 56, 218–26.

[44] B.L. Fredrickson and C. Branigan (2005). Positive emotions broaden the scope of attention and thought-action repertoires. *Cognition and Emotion*, 19, 313–32.

[45] B. Fredrickson and M. Losada (2005). Positive affect and the complex dynamics of human flourishing. *American Psychologist*, 60, 678–86.

[46] Ibid., p. 684.

[47] B.L. Fredrickson (2009). *Positivity: Groundbreaking research reveals how to embrace the hidden strength of positive emotions, overcome negativity, and thrive.* New York: Crown.

[48] M.W. Gallagher and S.J. Lopez (2007). Curiosity and well-being. *Journal of Positive Psychology*, 2, 236–48.

[49] Curiosity, an engine of well-being: An interview with Todd Kashdan. *Positive Psychology News Daily*, 21 April 2009.

[50] Robert A. Emmons and Michael E. McCullough (2003). Counting blessings versus burdens: An experimental investigation of gratitude and subjective well-being in daily life. *Journal of Personality and Social Psychology*, 84(2), 377–89.

[51] Ibid., p. 379.

[52] Sonja Lyubomirsky (2007). *The How of Happiness: The practical guide to getting the life you want.* London: Sphere, pp. 91–9.

[53] M. Seligman (2002). *Authentic Happiness: Using the new positive psychology to realize your potential for lasting fulfilment.* London: Free Press.

[54] Julia K. Boehm and Sonja Lyubomirsky (2008). *The Promise of Sustainable Happiness.* University of California, Riverside.

[55] K. Otake, S. Shimai, J. Tanaka-Matsumi, K. Otsui and B. Fredrickson (2006). Happy people become kinder through kindness: A counting kindness intervention. *Journal of Happiness Studies*, 7(3), 361–75.

[56] B.L. Fredrickson, M.A. Cohn, K.A. Coffey, J. Pek and S.M. Finkel (2008). Open hearts build lives: Positive emotions, induced through loving-kindness meditation, build consequential personal resources. *Journal of Personality and Social Psychology*, 95(5), 1045–62.

[57] B. Rimland (1982). The altruism paradox. *Psychological Reports*, 51, 521.

[58] D. Kahneman, A. B. Krueger, D. Schkade, N. Schwarz and A. A. Stone (2006). Would you be happier if you were richer? A focusing illusion. *Science*, 312 (5782), 1908–10.

59. J. Nakamura and M. Csikszentmihalyi (2005). The concept of flow. In C.R. Snyder and S.J. Lopez (eds), *Handbook of Positive Psychology*. Oxford: Oxford University Press, p. 90.

60. M. Csikzentmihalyi (2008). *Flow: The psychology of optimal experience*. New York: Harper Perennial.

61. F.B. Bryant and J. Veroff (2007). Savouring: *A new model of positive experience*. Mahwah, NJ: Lawrence Erlbaum Associates.

62. Ibid.

63. Martin E.P. Seligman (2003). *Authentic Happiness: Using the new positive psychology to realise your potential for lasting fulfilment*. London: Nicholas Brealey, p. 160.

64. Ibid., p. 133.

65. A. Linley, K.M. Nielsen, A.M. Wood, R. Gillett, and R. Biswas-Diener (2010). Using signature strengths in pursuit of goals: Effects on goal progress, need satisfaction, and well-being, and implications for coaching psychologists. *International Coaching Psychology Review*, 5(1), 6–15.

66. Tom Rath (2007). *Strengths Finder 2.0*. New York: Gallop Press, in connection with www.cliftonstrengthsfinder.com.

67. http://cappeu.com/realise2.htm.

68. M.E.P. Seligman, T. Steen, N. Park and C. Peterson (2005). Positive psychology progress: Empirical validation of interventions. *American Psychologist*, 60(5), 410–21.

69. K.M. Sheldon, A.J. Elliot, Y. Kim, and T. Kasser (2001). What is satisfying about satisfying events. *Journal of Personality and Social Psychology*, 80(2), 325–39.

70. The candle problem. See Barry Schwartz at www.tedtalks.com.

71. D. Simonton (2005). Creativity. In C.R. Snyder and S.J. Lopez (eds), *Handbook of Positive Psychology*. Oxford: Oxford University Press, p. 195.

72. Sheldon *et al.*, ibid., pp. 325–39.

73. R.M. Ryan and E.L. Deci (2000). Self-determination theory and the facilitation of intrinsic motivation, social development and well-being. *Journal of Personality and Social Psychology*, 79, 367–84.

74. C.R. Snyder, K.L. Rand and D.R. Sigmon (2005). Hope theory: A member of the positive psychology family. In C.R. Snyder and S.J. Lopez (eds), *Handbook of Positive Psychology*. Oxford: Oxford University Press, p. 258.

[75] Ibid., p. 258.

[76] J. Haidt (2005). *The Happiness Hypothesis: Finding modern truth in ancient wisdom.* New York: Basic Books, p. 17.

[77] S.J. Lopez, C.R. Snyder, J.L. Magyar-Moe, L.M. Edwards, J. Teramoto Pedrotti, K. Janowski, J.L. Turner and C. Pressgrove (2004). Strategies for accentuating hope. In P.A. Linley and S. Joseph (eds), *Positive Psychology in Practice.* Hoboken NJ: Wiley and Sons, p. 396.

[78] J. Maddux (2005). Self-efficacy: The power of believing you can. In C.R. Snyder and S.J. Lopez (eds), *Handbook of Positive Psychology.* Oxford: Oxford University Press, p. 278.

[79] A. Bandura (1977). Self-efficacy: Towards a unifying theory of behaviour change. *Psychological Review,* 84, 191–215.

[80] H. Gardner (1983). *Frames of mind: The theory of multiple intelligences.* New York: Basic Books.

[81] R.E. Boyatzis, D. Goleman, and K. Rhee (2000). Clustering competence in emotional intelligence: Insights from the Emotional Competence Inventory (ECI). In R. Bar-On and J. Parkers (eds), *The Handbook of Emotional Intelligence.* Hoboken, NJ: John Wiley and Sons, pp. 343–62.

[82] R. Bar-On (2000). Emotional and social intelligence: Insights from the Emotional Quotient Inventory. In R. Bar-On and J. Parker, ibid., pp. 374–81.

[83] J.D. Mayer, P. Salovey, and D.R. Caruso (2002). Mayer–Salovey–Caruso Emotional Intelligence Test (MSCEIT). Toronto, Ontario: Multi-Health Systems, Inc.

[84] J.D. Mayer, P. Salovey, and D.R. Caruso (2004). Emotional intelligence: Theory, findings and implications. *Psychological Inquiry,* 15(3), 199; J.D. Mayer, D.R. Caruso and P. Salovey (2000). Selecting a measure of emotional intelligence: The case for ability scales. In Bar-On and Parker, ibid., pp. 329–42.

[85] Paul Ekman (1972). Universals and cultural differences in facial expressions of emotion. In J. Cole (ed.), *Nebraska Symposium on Motivation 1971* (vol. 19). Lincoln, NE: University of Nebraska Press, pp. 207–83.

[86] D.A. Bernstein, A. Clarke-Stewart, L.A. Penner, E.J. Roy, and C.D. Wickens (2000). *Psychology* (5th edn). Boston, MA: Houghton Mifflin.

87. S.F. Davis and J.J. Palladino (2000). *Psychology* (3rd edn). Upper Saddle River, NJ: Prentice-Hall.

88. A.M. Isen, A.S. Rosenzweig, and M.J. Young (1991). The influence of positive affect on clinical problem solving. *Medical Decision Making,* 11, 221–7; A. Isen (2001). An influence of positive affect on decision making in complex situations: Theoretical issues with practical implications. *Journal of Consumer Psychology,* 11(2), 75–85.

89. E. Eich, D. Macauley and L. Ryan (1994). Mood dependent memory for events of the personal past. *Journal of Experimental Psychology: General,* 123, 201–15.

90. R. Plutchik. (1980), Emotion: Theory, research, and experience: Vol. 1. Theories of emotion, 1, New York: Academic.

91. Alan Carr (2004). *Positive Psychology: The science of happiness and human strength.* London: Routledge, p. 142.

92. S.E. Taylor and J.D. Brown (1988). Illusion and wellbeing; A social psychological perspective on mental health. *Psychological Bulletin,* 103(2), 193–210.

93. J. Haidt (2005), ibid.

94. J. Gray (1992). *Men are from Mars, Women are from Venus. New York:* Harper Collins.

95. Alan Carr, ibid., pp. 78–81.

96. R.E. Lucas, A.E. Clark, Y. Georgellis and E. Diener (2003). Reexamining adaption and the set point model of happiness: Reactions to changes in marital status. *Journal of Personality and Social Psychology,* 84, 527–39.

97. L. Harker and D. Kelter (2001). Expressions of positive emotion in women's college yearbook pictures and their relationship to personality and life outcomes across adulthood. *Journal of Personality and Social Psychology,* 80, 112–24.

98. V.G. Lewis and D.L. Borders (1995). Life satisfaction of single middle-aged professional women. *Journal of Counseling and Development,* 74, 93–100.

99. John Gottmann (1994). *Why Marriages Succeed or Fail and How You Can Make Yours Last.* New York: Simon and Schuster.

100. Marcus Aurelius (1997). *Meditations.* Ware, Herts: Wordsworth Editions, p. 54.

101. J. Bowlby (1988). *A Secure Base: Parent-child attachment and healthy human development*. New York: Basic Books.

102. Carr (2004), ibid., pp. 125–6.

103. Carr (2004), ibid., p. 126.

104. S.L. Gable, H.T. Reis, E.A. Impett and E.R. Asher (2004). What do you do when things go right? The intrapersonal and interpersonal benefits of sharing positive events. *Journal of Personality and Social Psychology*, 87(2), 228–45.

105. B. Schwartz (2004). Doing better but feeling worse. In P.A. Linley and S. Joseph (eds), *Positive Psychology in Practice*. Hoboken, NJ: John Wiley and Sons, p. 97.

106. S. Lyubormirsky, K.L. Tucker and F. Kasri (2001). Responses to hedonically conflicting social comparisons: Comparing happy and unhappy individuals. *European Journal of Social Psychology*, 31, 1–25.

107. S.R. Lyubomirsky and L. Ross (1997). Hedonic consequences of social comparison: A contrast of happy and unhappy people. *Journal of Personality and Social Psychology*, 73(6), 1141–57.

108. O. James (2007). *Affluenza*. London: Random House.

109. You can see Victor Frankl at www.ted.com/talks/viktor_frankl_youth_in_search_of_meaning.html.

110. K.J. Klob and L. Jussim (1994). Teacher expectations and under-achieving gifted children. *Roeper Review*, 17(1), 26–30.

111. J. Campbell (2009) *Resilience: personal and organisational*, Edinburgh: lifetimeswork.

112. Ann S. Masten and J. Douglas Coatsworth (1998). The development of competence in favorable and unfavorable environment: Lessons from research on successful children. *American Psychologist*, 53, 205–20.

113. M.E.P. Seligman (2006). *Learned Optimism: How to change your mind and your life*. First Vintage Books edn. New York: Random House, p. 111.

114. Shelly E. Taylor and Jonathan Brown (1998). Illusion and wellbeing: A social psychological perspective on mental health. *Psychological Bulletin*, 103(2), 193–210.

115. M.E.P. Seligman and S.F. Maier (1967). Failure to escape traumatic shock. *Journal of Experimental Psychology*, 74, 1–9.

116. L.Y. Abramson, M.E.P. Seligman, and J.D. Teasdale (1978). Learned helplessness in humans: Critique and reformulation. *Journal of Abnormal Psychology*, 87, 49–74.

117. A.T. Beck (1976). *Cognitive Therapy and the Emotional Disorders.* New York: International Universities Press; A. Ellis and R. Harper (1975). *A New Guide to Rational Living* (rev. edn). Hollywood, CA: Wilshire Books.

118. You can find this at www.authentichappiness.com.

119. M.E.P. Seligman (2006), ibid., p 40.

120. Ibid., p. 259.

121. See K. Reivich and A. Shatte (2002). *The Resilience Factor.* New York: Broadway Books, pp. 137–44 if you want to know more about this subject.

122. Ibid.

123. C. Carver and M. Scheier (2005). Optimism. In C.R. Snyder and S.J. Lopez (eds), *Handbook of Positive Psychology.* Oxford: Oxford University Press, p. 235.

124. M. Scheier, C. Carver, and W. Bridges (2002). Optimism, pessimism and psychological wellbeing. In Edward C. Chang (ed.), *Optimism and pessimism: Implications for theory research and practice.* Washington, DC: American Psychological Association, p. 193.

125. Carver and Scheier, ibid.

126. D. Watson, L.A. Clark, and G. Carey (1988). Positive and negative affect and their relation to anxiety and depressive disorders. *Journal of Abnormal Psychology,* 97, 346–53.

127. G.L. Garamoni, C.F. Reynolds, M.E. Thase, E. Frank, and A.L. Fasiczka (1992). Shifts in affective balance during therapy of major depression. *Consulting and Clinical Psychology,* 60, 260–6.

128. Julie Norem (2002). Defensive pessimism, optimism and pessimism. In Edward C. Chang (ed.), *Optimism and pessimism: Implications for theory research and practice.* Washington, DC: American Psychological Association, pp. 87–90.

129. G.E. Vaillant (2000). Adaptive mental mechanisms: Their role in positive psychology. *American Psychologist,* 55(1), 89–98.

130. H. Lefcourt (2005). Humour. In C.R. Snyder and S.J. Lopez (eds), *Handbook of Positive Psychology.* Oxford: Oxford University Press, p. 619–31, quoting S.E. Thomas (2001). *An investigation into the use of humour for coping with stress.* Unpublished.

131. Ibid., p. 622; D. Zillmann, and S.H. Stocking (1976). Putdown humour. *Journal of Communication,* 26, 154–63.

132. R.G. Tedeschi and L.G. Calhoun (2006). A clinical approach to post traumatic growth. In P.A. Linley and S. Joseph (eds), *Positive Psychology in Practice*. Hoboken, NJ: John Wiley and Sons, p. 406–7.

133. S. Nolen-Hoeksema and C. Davis (2005). Positive responses to loss. In C.R. Snyder and S.J. Lopez (eds), *Handbook of Positive Psychology*. Oxford: Oxford University Press, p. 602.

134. Tedeschi and Calhoun (2006), ibid., p. 406–7.

135. See K.G. Niederhoffer and J.W. Pennebaker (2005). Sharing one's story: On the benefits of writing or talking about emotional experience. In C.R. Snyder and S.J. Lopez (eds), *Handbook of Positive Psychology*. Oxford: Oxford University Press, pp. 573–83.

136. Ibid., p. 574.

137. A.J. Sameroff (ed.) (2009). *The Transactional Model of Development: How children and contexts shape each other*. Washington, DC: American Psychological Association.

138. J. Garbino and R.H.A. Haslam (2005). Lost boys: Why our sons turn violent and how we can save them. *Paediatrics and Child Health*, 10(8), 447–50.

139. R.F. Baumeister and K.D. Vohs (2005). Meaningfulness in life. In C.R. Snyder and S.J. Lopez (eds), *Handbook of Positive Psychology*. Oxford: Oxford University Press, p. 614.

140. V. Frankl (2004). Man's Search for Meaning. New York: Random House and London: Rider, p. 111.

141. Patricia A. Boyle, Aron S. Buchman, Lisa L. Barnes and David A. Bennett (2010). Effect of a purpose in life on risk of incident Alzheimer disease and mild cognitive impairment in community-dwelling older persons. *Archives of General Psychiatry*, 67(3), 304–10.

142. L. Sagiv, S. Roccas and O. Hazan (2004). Value pathways to well-being: Healthy values, valued goal attainment and environmental congruence. In P.A. Linley and S. Joseph (eds), *Positive Psychology in Practice*. Hoboken, NJ: John Wiley and Sons, pp. 68–84.

143. Susan Harter (2005). Authenticity. In C.R. Snyder and S.J. Lopez (eds), *Handbook of Positive Psychology*. Oxford: Oxford University Press, p. 390.

144. O. James, ibid.

145. Max Weber (1905). *The Protestant Work Ethic and 'The Spirit of Capitalism'* (trans. Stephen Kalberg, 2002). Los Angeles, CA: Roxbury, pp. 19 and 35.

146. You can find Steve Pavlina at www.stevepavlina.com/blog/2005/01/how-to-discover-your-life-purpose-in-about-20-minutes/.

147. Sagiv, Roccas and Hozan, ibid., p. 77.

148. Tim Kasser (2006). Materialism and its alternatives. In M. Csikszentmihalyi and I.S. Csikszentmihalyi (eds), *A Life Worth Living*. Oxford: Oxford University Press, pp. 203–4.

149. Ibid., p. 203.

150. Ibid., p. 205.

151. David Watson (2005). Positive affectivity: The disposition to experience pleasurable emotional states. In C.R. Snyder and S.J. Lopez (eds), *Handbook of Positive Psychology*. Oxford: Oxford University Press, p. 113.

152. A. Reznitskaya and R. Sternberg (2004). Teaching students to make wise judgements: The teaching for wisdom program. In P.A. Linley and S. Joseph (eds), *Positive Psychology in Practice*. Hoboken, NJ: John Wiley and Sons, p. 188.

153. You can see Barry Schwartz talking about wisdom at www.ted.com/talks/lang/eng/barry_schwartz_on_our_loss_of_wisdom.

154. P. Baltes (2005). The psychology of wisdom: Theoretical and empirical challenges. In R.J. Sternberg and J. Jordan (eds), *A Handbook of Wisdom: Psychological perspectives*. Cambridge: Cambridge University Press, p. 112.

155. U.M. Staudinger, C. Mickler, and J. Dörner (2005). Wisdom and personality. In R.J. Sternberg and J. Jordan (eds), *A Handbook of Wisdom: Psychological perspectives*. Cambridge: Cambridge University Press.

156. R. Sternberg (1998). A balance theory of wisdom. *Review of General Psychology*, 2(4), 346–65.

157. June Price Tangney (2005). Humility. In C.R. Snyder and S.J. Lopez (eds), *Handbook of Positive Psychology*. Oxford: Oxford University Press, pp. 412–14.

158. U. Kunzman and P. Baltes (2005). The psychology of wisdom: Theoretical and empirical challenges. In R.J. Sternberg and J. Jordan (eds), *A Handbook of Wisdom: Psychological perspectives*. Cambridge: Cambridge University Press, p. 123.

159. Charlotte Style (2009, in press). The effect of group-based life coaching on happiness and well-being.

160. S. Bluck and J. Gluck (2005). From the inside out: People's implicit theories of wisdom. In R.J. Sternberg and J. Jordan (eds), *A Handbook of Wisdom: Psychological perspectives*. Cambridge: Cambridge University Press, p. 92.

161. Ibid., p. 92.

162. D. Watson (2005). Positive affectivity. In C.R. Snyder and S.J. Lopez (eds), *Handbook of Positive Psychology*. Oxford: Oxford University Press, p. 113.

163. David Myers (2000). The funds, friends and faith of happy people. *American Psychologist*, 55(1), 56–67.

164. K. Pargament and A. Mahoney (2005). Spirituality: Discovering and conserving the sacred. In C.R. Snyder and S.J. Lopez (eds), *Handbook of Positive Psychology*. Oxford: Oxford University Press, p. 647.

165. Ibid., p. 647.

166. Robert Emmons (2006). Spirituality: Recent progress. In M. Csikszentmihalyi, and I.S. Csikszentmihalyi (eds), *A Life Worth Living*. Oxford: Oxford University Press, p. 203–4.

167. Ibid., p. 75.

168. C.T. Coyle, and R.D. Enright (1997). Forgiveness intervention with postabortion men. *Journal of Consulting and Clinical Psychology*, 65, 1042–46.

169. Freedman, S.R. (1999). A voice of forgiveness: One incest survivor's experience forgiving her father. *Journal of Family Psychotherapy*, 10, 37–60.

170. Emmons, ibid., p. 75.

171. J.C. Karremans, P.A.M. Van Lange, J.W. Ouwerkerk and E.S. Kluwer (2003). When forgiving enhances psychological well-being: The role of interpersonal commitment. *Journal of Personality and Social Psychology*, 84, 1011–26.

172. Roy Baumeister.

173. H.H. Dalai Lama and Howard Cutler (1998). *The Art of Happiness: A handbook for living*. London: Coronet books, Hodder and Stoughton.

174. S.L. Shapiro, G.E. Schwartz, and C. Santerre (2005). Meditation and positive psychology. In C.R. Snyder and S.J. Lopez (eds), *Handbook of Positive Psychology*. New York: Oxford University Press, p. 632.

175. E. Langer (2005). Wellbeing: Mindfulness versus positive evaluation. In C.R. Snyder and S.J. Lopez (eds), *Handbook of Positive Psychology*. Oxford: Oxford University Press, p. 222, referencing E. Langer, E. Marcatonis and S. Golub (2000). *No Regrets: The ameliorative affect of mindfulness*. Unpublished.

176. P. Brickman, D. Coates and R. Janoff-Bulman (1978). Lottery winners and accident victims: Is happiness relative? *Journal of Personality and Social Psychology*, 36, 917–27.

177. M. Babyak, J.A. Blumenthal, S. Herman, P. Khatri, M. Doraiswamy, K. Moore, W.E. Craighead, T.T Baldewicz and K.R Krishnan (2000). Exercise treatment for major depression: maintenance of therapeutic benefit at 10 months. *Psychosomatic Medicine*, 62 (5), 633–8.

178. S.J. Biddle, K.R. Fox and S.H. Boutcher (eds) (2000). *Physical Activity and Psychological Wellbeing*. London: Routledge.

179. F. H. Gage (2002). Neurogenesis in the adult brain. *The Journal of Neuroscience*, 22(3), 612–13.

180. L. Hoggard (2005). *How to Be Happy*. London: BBC Books.

181. Alia J. Crum and Ellen J. Langer (2007). Mind-set matters: Exercise and the placebo effect. *Psychological Science*, 18, 165–71.

182. K. Graham, A. Massak, A. Demers and J. Rehm (2007). Does the association between alcohol consumption and depression depend on how they are measured *Alcoholism: Clinical and Experimental Research*, 13(1), 78–88.

183. E. N. Meilahn (1995). Low serum cholesterol: hazardous to health? *Circulation*, 92, 2365–6; C. Iribarren, D.M. Reed, R. Chen, K. Yano and J.H. Dwyer (1995). Low cholesterol and mortality: which is the cause and which is the effect? *Circulation*, 92, 2396–2403.

184. R. Craddick (1961). Size of Santa Claus drawings as a function of time before and after Christmas. *Journal of Psychological Studies*, 12, 121–5.

185. S. Kim and J. Kim (2007). Mood after various brief exercise and sport modes: aerobics, hip-hop dancing, and body conditioning. *Perceptual Motor Skills*, 104(3), 1265–70.

186. M. Smith, S., Draper, C., Potter and C. Burke (2008). *Energy cost of rock drumming*. Thirteenth Annual Congress of European College of Sport Science, Estoril, Portugal, 9–12 July.

187. Susan Hallam (2010). The power of music: its impact on the intellectual, social and personal development of children and young people. Retrieved 7 August 2010 from www.ioe.ac.uk/Year_of_Music.pdf.

188. Richard M. Ryan, Netta Weinstein, Jessey Bernstein, Kirk Warren Brown, Louis Mistretta, Marylène Gagné (2010). Vitalizing effects of being outdoors and in nature. *Journal of Environmental Psychology*, 30(2), 159.

189. S.T. Lindau, L.P. Schumm, E.O. Laumann, *et al.* (2007). A study of sexuality and health among older adults in the United States. *New England Journal of Medicine*, 357(8), 762–74.

190. K.M. Grewen, B.J. Anderson, S.S. Girdler, and K.C. Light (2003). Warm partner contact is related to lower cardiovascular reactivity. *Behavioural Medicine*, 29(3), 123–30.

191. V. Lewis and D. Borders (1995). Life satisfaction of single middle-aged professional women. *Journal of Counseling and Development*, 74, 93–100.

192. Jim Loehr, Tony Schwartz and James Loehr (2004). *The Power of Full Engagement.* New York: Simon and Schuster.

193. T. Ben-Shahar (2008). *Happier: Can you learn to be happy?* Maidenhead: McGraw Hill, p. 9.

194. J.K. Harter, F.L. Schmidt and C.L. Keyes (2002). Well-being in the Workplace and its Relationship to Business Outcomes: A review of the Gallup Studies. In C.L. Keyes and J. Haidt (eds), *Flourishing: The positive person and the good life.* Washington, D.C.: American Psychological Association, pp. 205–24.

195. Ibid.

196. N. Turner, J. Barling and A. Zacharatos (2005). Positive psychology at work. In C.R. Snyder and S.J. Lopez (eds), *Handbook of Positive Psychology.* Oxford: Oxford University Press, p. 719.

197. Gallup (2002). Ibid.

198. J. Collins (2001). *Good to Great: Why some companies make the leap ... and others don't.* New York: HarperCollins.

199. Carol Dweck (2006). Mindset: The new psychology of success. New York: Ballantine books, p. 140.

200. Referred to by Carol Dweck, ibid., p. 111.

201. Gallup (2002). Ibid.

202. J. Harter, F. Schmidt and C. Keyes (2002). Wellbeing in the workplace and its relationship to business outcomes: A review of the Gallup studies. In C. Keyes and J. Haidt (eds), *Flourishing: The positive person and the life well-lived*. Washington DC: American Psychological Association, pp. 205–24.

203. N. Turner, J. Barling and A. Zacharatos (2002). Positive psychology at work. In C.R. Snyder and S.J. Lopez (eds), *Handbook of Positive Psychology*. Oxford: Oxford University Press, p. 719.

204. See J. Ludema, D. Whitney, B. Mohr and T. Griffin (2003). *The Appreciative Inquiry Summit*. San Francisco, CA: Berrett-Koehler.

205. Gallup (2002). Ibid.

206. L. Sagiv, S. Roccas and O. Hazan (2004). Value pathways to wellbeing: Healthy values, valued goal attainment and environmental congruence. In P.A. Linley and S. Joseph (eds), *Positive Psychology in Practice*. Hoboken, NJ: John Wiley and Sons, p. 75.

207. You can see Ken Robinson talking at www.tedtalks.com.

208. Turner, Barling, and Zacharatos (2005), ibid., p. 721.

209. Ibid., p. 725.

210. You can see Stephen Wolfran at www.tedtalks.com.

211. The origins of this proverb are not fully known; it is often attributed to Richard the Third. See Wikipedia for information.

212. For Socrates and Aristotle, knowledge stands above all the virtues.

213. Roy F. Baumeister, Jennifer D. Campbell, Joachim I. Krueger and Kathleen D. Vohs (2003). Does high self-esteem cause better performance, interpersonal success, happiness, or healthier lifestyles? *American Psychological Society*, 4(1), p. 1–44.

Index